CW00525509

Prayer for an Infidel

Memories from Afghanistan

Eileen Masters

ISBN 978-1-291-61557-9

Published in 2013 by Eileen Masters
Enquiries to eileen@eileenmasters.net

Also available as an eBook ISBN 978-1-291-61587-6

THANK YOU

Michael Semple for the time we worked together, your kind approach to resolving our miscommunications, and for providing a postscript to this memoir

Ahmad Zia Langari (Zia) for keeping me safe many times and contributing a postscript to this book

Alastair Walker for your help with crafting scenes that bring my diary notes to life

Rosemary Bartholomew for copy-editing and proofreading

Hastings Writers' Group for your feedback on the work in progress

Jon and Magda, Dan and Mandy, for encouraging me along the way

Alan for keeping the home fires burning and retaining our letters on which, together with my diaries, this book is based

Everyone I mention in this book, and everyone who reads it, for sharing with me the experience of a lifetime.

Cover image: Waiting at Kabul airport November 1992
Photo taken by Ahmad Zia Langari

*Our bags are stuffed with Afghani notes, enough to turn our
rucksacks and shopping bags into handy seats while we wait.*
Page 184

CONTENTS

PREFACE

As NATO prepares for the withdrawal of its fighting troops from Afghanistan and our television and radio newscasts speak of Kabul, Mazar-i-Sharif and other faraway places, my memory returns to my visit to Afghanistan over twenty years ago. At that time, a different kind of war was raging.

It was three months after the fall of the Soviet-backed Najibullah government and Rabbani was president of Afghanistan. His government was unstable and the situation quickly descended into multi-factional conflict. It was in the hot ground of the ensuing civil war that the seeds of the Taliban were to germinate and grow, as the Taliban promised the war-weary Afghan people a way out of the horrors of conflict.

In 1992 I was working for Oxfam, the international aid agency. My husband and I had previously worked in Pakistan for six years. When the opportunity arose to revisit the region that I loved, it was quite impossible for me not to volunteer to go. On 18th July 1992, the day of our twenty-second wedding anniversary, I travelled into Kabul. I had failed, however, to update myself on the security situation. Although I did not know it, the city was under a heavy bombardment and many aid agencies had already evacuated their non-essential staff.

These chapters are my personal recollections of that time, punctuated by letters from home and echoed in my childhood memories.

Sometimes, I have forgotten the names of people I met and have invented names for them, attributed words to people that communicate the gist of what was said but which may not be the exact words they used, and moved some scenes to where they will make sense to the reader rather than the date on which they occurred. Sometimes, to avoid repetition, I have drawn a number of similar experiences into one scene. With these literary liberties, the account is true to my recollections.

I may be mistaken, at times, in my understanding of what took place but it is the memory I have, told from my point of view and accepting that others will have seen it differently.

I particularly wish to record my great respect for Michael Semple who began Oxfam's work in Afghanistan in 1989 and is now a leading international authority on Afghanistan, and that we resolved our miscommunications amicably in the years that followed the events of this book.

I pay special tribute to the women of Afghanistan who, mostly invisible to Western eyes, bear the greater part of the suffering of conflict.

Finally, I wish to express the high regard that I have for the international aid agency Oxfam and the work that it carries out in the most difficult places on earth.

Eileen Masters
October 2013

CHAPTER 1: A STRANGE PLACE TO PICNIC

Saturday 18th July 1992, somewhere on the road to Kabul

It's nine years and seven weeks before 9/11 on the day I'm travel-sick in the Khyber Pass and I'm in big trouble. Normally I look strangers in the eye, extend my right hand and say, 'Eileen Masters, Oxfam.' Not this time. These guys only shake hands with men and Kalashnikovs. I let Zia, the driver, do the talking.

Zia is 'Mr Fix It'. Whatever you need, from a house to rent to project supplies or letters of safe passage, he knows someone who will supply it. The question is can he fix this? I enjoy something exciting to get the adrenalin flowing, to heighten the senses, attempting something few others would dare to do. Is this a risk too far, a challenge too many? I take a deep breath to calm my racing heartbeat and hide my hands under my *chador* shawl so no-one will see them shaking.

Yesterday, Zia came to the Islamabad office in Pakistan to pick me up and drive me to my posting in Kabul, Afghanistan. He's late thirties, I'd guess, with a short, black beard and moustache. His flat *pekol* cap tells me he's Pashtun. His crisp, white shirt and smart, western-style trousers say he has a mother or a wife at home to iron his clothes every morning. He speaks English, which means he's well educated and used to working with foreigners.

'Suzuki is too clean,' Zia explains, daubing the pick-up's gleaming, white paintwork with mud. 'If looks new, they will steal it. In Afghanistan is better to look poor.'

Michael Semple comes to see us off. Michael is my boss. He established Oxfam's work in Afghanistan virtually single-handedly, cross-border and often cross-line. He's dressed in a neat *shalwar* suit. His blue eyes seem deeply troubled.

I've had a short briefing from Michael. He had spoken quietly with a trace of an Irish accent.

'It's peaceful now. They've called a ceasefire. Refugees are returning to Kabul. When I drove through last month, families were having picnics in the Khyber Pass.'

It seems to me a strange place to picnic but I have to accept that I've been in the U.K. for the last three years and things do change.

'I want to arrange a workshop in Kabul for the Pakistani staff. They do so much to support the programmes in Afghanistan, it would be good for them to visit. Make arrangements for them to come during the last week of August.'

'OK,' I'd said, 'sounds good.'

It's time to leave. Zia removes his cap, bows his head and says the *Bismillah,* a prayer for Allah's mercy, and with a final round of goodbyes we set off for Kabul.

Now, this is 18th July 1992, I'm talking about and me in *shalwar kameez* under a cotton *chador*-shawl. We're sitting on seats that are over the engine and hot enough to fry eggs on, no air-conditioning and the weather at gas mark four.

The Khyber Pass will take us thirty-five miles to the Pakistan-Afghanistan border at Torkham, between mountain-sides that have a thousand eyes. I remember our trip here with my husband and sons in 1983. It was scalding hot then too. The Russians occupied Afghanistan at that time. A guide took us up into a narrow mountain road. He told us this was the path the Afghan freedom fighters took over the mountains and into Afghanistan. He said that the Russians didn't know about this path and Afghan people could safely come and go. We looked down at the Russian soldiers guarding the border. Our guide wouldn't take us any further. The rest of the way was an Afghan secret. He showed us the hideouts of the Afghan resistance fighters, the Mujahedeen, in caves carved into the hot, rocky mountainsides high above the pass. Freedom fighters could live for weeks here with just their string beds, rifles and water containers, watching every movement along the road below, guarding the entrance to their homeland.

Going up into the Khyber Pass isn't too bad. The engine groans and the gears grind a bit but it's OK. Coming down is something else. Zia knows the Khyber Pass like his own backyard and he's swirling the pick-up round the bends, spinning down like a fairground ride. I know I'm not going to keep my stomach contents in.

'Zia, can we stop for a moment, please?'

'No, sorry Mrs Eileen, is not possible here.'

I lean my head out of the window and throw up. I'm feeling really stupid now. Zia looks at me from the corner of his eye. I hate being the feeble female.

My mother's words return to haunt me. 'Your father doesn't love you. He's disappointed you weren't a boy.'

I take a Kwell travel pill from my handbag and swallow it down with a sip from my water bottle.

Go away, Mother, I'm as good as any boy.

Zia drives on into the middle of nowhere and finally stops for a break at a roadside cluster of shed-like shops. I climb out of the Suzuki, my feet stirring up a pool in the hot sand. I stand holding onto the open door feeling disoriented, nauseous and wobbly, my clothes wet with sweat.

Zia goes to a stall and returns with two small bottles. 'Here is danger. Must not stay long,' he whispers, handing me a Sprite.

I wipe the dust from my eyes with the corner of my *duppatta* scarf. Through the blur of my travel-sick vision, I see his eyes are alert, scanning our surroundings.

The Sprite relieves my nausea for the moment. I wonder how long it will stay down? I'd like a bit longer but Zia is getting back into the driver's seat, his face tense, his eyes watchful. I climb back into the cab of the little pick-up. Through my clothes, the seat feels hot underneath me. A dusty boy takes our empty bottles back to the stall. Zia starts the engine.

We travel on until we reach the border. Zia goes inside the building with our passports and papers. I stand outside holding onto a tamarisk tree, trying to restore my sense of balance under its cool shade.

Fortune smiles on me and it takes an age for Zia to complete his negotiations with the border officials, some problem with the paperwork, apparently. By the time he returns, my sips of water are staying down and my stomach seems to be settling.

We continue through the Torkham gate border that divides Pakistan from Afghanistan. On the Pakistan side we were in tribal territory, outside the jurisdiction of the Pakistani government, and we enjoyed a flirtation with danger. On the Afghan side we drive into a shroud of foreboding. Signs in English and Farsi warn of landmines. The landscape becomes barren, scattered with the debris of war.

There's not much left of the road. It's been shelled, bombed and heavily mined, first by the Russians and then the warring Mujahedeen factions. Zia manages the pick-up through the slippery sand, up, down and around the craters, keeping in the tracks of earlier vehicles. Hopefully, if they didn't hit a mine, we won't.

I look out at the burned-out tanks and deserted, mud-brick villages strewn across the desolate landscape.

'Russians. They burned our villages. We burned their tanks.'

I shudder at the thought of so much suffering.

'Zia, how many people work at the Kabul office?'

'There is Nafisa. She keeps office records and cares for money. Ehsan, he helps me in refugee programmes.'

'Is there a *chowkidar?*'

'Yes, is *chowkidar* for night-time and two daytime guards. There is also Gulshad, she cleans and...'

CRACK!

The sound of gunfire behind us. CRACK! CRACK! CRACK!

'Zia, are they firing at us?' I ask, as calmly as I can manage. Zia mustn't think I'm panicking.

'Your face hide.'

I pull my shawl across my nose and mouth. The gunfire stops.

We meet a convoy of colourful trucks coming in the opposite direction, laden with people and their household belongings. The men are a pool of grey clothing capped with checked turbans. The women, in all-covering blue *burqas,* clasp their children in their arms and between their knees.

'They leave Kabul,' Zia says, 'because of shelling.'

'Michael said there's a ceasefire and people are returning to Kabul. He said families are having picnics in the Khyber Pass.'

'Kabul is shelling two weeks now. Many are leaving. No picnics.' He chuckles at the thought.

I feel foolish.

'There is problem. Some travel home to Kabul because they hear there is peace now. Others leaving because of new shelling. It is chaos. Everyone is on road travelling the both ways.'

I offer Zia a bottle of water. He hasn't brought any food or water. Every year, throughout the holy month of Ramadan, he doesn't eat, drink or smoke from dawn to dusk no matter what the weather. To him, an eight-hour journey in ferocious heat doesn't require such sustenance. I prefer my driver not to be dehydrated. Zia drinks from the bottle with one hand, steering the little Suzuki with the other. I pass him biscuits, one at a time from the packet, so he can concentrate on driving.

'What do you do at the Kabul office, Zia?'

'I am Programme Manager for refugees returning from Pakistan. When they are to arrive Mr Michael sends me...'

They jump out from the sides of the road and aim their rifles at us, six armed men with black beards, dressed in black turbans and grey *shalwar* suits. They hop up onto the pick-up and perch behind Zia, their guns pointing at his head.

I can't take it in. It feels unreal, like watching a film projected in 3D all around me.

The gunmen shout at Zia in Pashto. We slowly turn off the road. We're not in the vehicle tracks now. I hope these guys remember where they laid the mines and are in a mood to avoid them.

We turn and drive toward a fortress. Massive, wooden gates open. Urged on by the guns, we enter. The doors bang closed behind us. In front of us there's a pair of iron gates. We go through. Another loud clang.

We've been made to disappear.

Zia stays in the driver's seat, his hands on the steering wheel. He sits very still. He doesn't make a single movement until the men come over and signal with their guns that he's to get out of the vehicle. He smiles, moving slowly, as you might approach a frightened horse. He greets them with a right-fist-on-heart salute. His body language seems deliberately relaxed. Only his eyes tell me he's on his guard.

The heat in the cab is stifling. As Zia and the gunmen move away from the vehicle, I open the passenger door, swivel round and sit sideways on. An L-shaped building encloses two sides of the courtyard. I look up, searching for any sight of women, children, chickens, goats, any signs of everyday life. There are none that I can see, only the eerie stillness of a deserted habitation. Iron-barred lock-ups line the third side of the courtyard. Is that where they'll keep us? What are the chances of someone finding us? A plain-looking white woman with rabbit teeth, wearing Pakistani clothes and accompanied by an Afghan man in a western shirt and trousers should have been conspicuous enough. We've been through the border crossing. Someone should be able to trace us.

Zia takes a packet of cigarettes out of his pocket and casually offers them round. I don't speak Pashto, though I can understand a little. I concentrate hard to make out Zia's words.

'*Huh!*' I hear him say, 'No such luck, you won't get any money for her. She's my wife. Her family don't want her because she's simple in the head. *Inshallah,* the marriage will get me a visa for America.'

'Why aren't you keeping her in *purdah?*'

'I'm taking her to my village. *Inshallah*, my mother will teach her everything.'

Oxfam doesn't pay ransoms. How long will I survive the heat, dirty water and malarial mosquitoes? Will they respect Zia's assertion that I'm his wife or do it anyway and make him watch? No, I mustn't let my thoughts go there. I have to keep calm. My survival may depend on my ability to think. I must keep a clear head, focus on what they are saying. Perhaps I should go over and demand to know what's going on?

I snatch a glance around. They're standing in a circle smoking Zia's cigarettes. He speaks. They all chuckle. Zia grins.

No. He's already cutting through the tension, gaining their trust, convincing them he's on their side. I'll leave the negotiations to him.

It seems like an age before Zia saunters back to the Suzuki. He looks at me and then toward our pick-up. I understand. I get back into the passenger seat. He sits at the wheel and turns the ignition. The engine bursts into life. Zia slowly turns the

Suzuki to face the entrance. Two gunmen are opening the inner gates. I mustn't hope yet. We drive cautiously through. The inner iron doors clang shut behind us. I crush the rising expectation of release, it's still too soon. Now they're opening the outer wooden gates. Even while he's driving, Zia's movements are slow, deliberately unthreatening.

We're out! Two gunmen escort us along the road for two miles and then jump off onto the dusty road.

I suddenly feel thirsty and reach for my water bottle. I gulp down three mouthfuls, no more. There's still a long way to go.

'What was all that about, Zia?'

'They think you are doctor. They want you to treat their wounded and...'

'And?'

Zia hesitates. 'Nothing, Mrs Eileen, nothing.'

The road to Kabul seems endless. Eventually, the landscape becomes suburbs and the suburbs merge into a city. The sun is setting. Dusk is my favourite time of day. It speaks of completion, arrival, the day's journey ended, the work done.

CRACK!

A single rifle shot over our heads. Anywhere, in any language, that means, 'STOP NOW!' Zia jams on the brakes. There's another teeth-clenching moment as a gang of armed men close in around us and peer through the open windows. They stare at me, their eyes filled with curiosity. It seems the group wants to requisition the Suzuki. Zia tells them he is only delivering the foreign lady doctor to her office. He would like to help them but we've had a long journey and there's very little fuel left. We have barely enough petrol to reach our street just over there. The gang leader waves us by.

'Office is on next street,' says Zia.

At last, the road in which the Oxfam building stands, a bungalow that serves both as the office and my accommodation, is moments away. A cup of tea is almost within reach. We turn the corner. In the evening darkness, it takes a moment for me to take in what it is. Then I figure out the shape of a blockade across the road. Youths, fully armed with rifles and shoulder-weapons are guarding the entrance to our street. Some of them are only boys who look barely ten or twelve years old. They're holding guns almost as big as they are. I'm more disconcerted by children with guns than by armed adults because youngsters may not understand the consequences of their actions.

Fear turns to resentful defiance. I want to say, 'Look, we've been travelling for fifteen hours. I need the bathroom and a cup of tea. Put those stupid weapons down and let us through.' I don't, of course. I sit quietly as Zia starts his negotiations again.

It's after eight in the evening when they let us into the Oxfam compound. Zia parks the Suzuki, removes the sparkplugs to disable it and we go indoors. The night watchman brings glasses of tea. I get through several refills before going to my private room. Exhausted, I lie on my bed.

Then it starts. The building shakes and the windows rattle as artillery shells crash down from the Kabul hills. Rockets boom, whistle, are momentarily silent, then explode. Outside my window a scream of agony sings a macabre song in the darkness. I get up and press my spare bedding into the window recess in case a shock of air sends the glass into a shower of diamond-sharp razors.

Still fully dressed so I shan't be embarrassed if they have to dig me out, my passport inside my underwear so they can identify my body, and the office walkie-talkie in my hand in case I wake up under a pile of rubble, I lie on my bed.

I hover in the haze between restless sleep and wakefulness. Somewhere in my mind the thunder of the artillery shells becomes the rolling booms from London's Royal Albert Dock that I heard long ago at our home in Silvertown and, in the chaos of the night, I'm a child again.

1953, Silvertown, East London, U.K.

'Stay where I can see you and don't spoil that frock, my girl, or you'll get what for!'

That was Mummy. *What for. Shout, shout, SHOUT.*

This was my favourite place. Up were bright colours, yellow sunflowers, blue sky, white clouds. Down were dark colours, green stems, leaves, muddy earth sticking to my shoes. *Squelch.*

I was four years old. I talked a lot. I knew because I heard Mummy talking to the nurse who brought my baby sister.

'Trouble is, Nurse, she rabbits nineteen to the dozen when there's no one there. She even argues with herself sometimes.'

'Don't worry, Mrs Hayward. Younger children often have imaginary friends. She'll grow out of it when baby Kathleen is old enough for her to play with.'

Imaginary. It was a nice word. What did it mean?

That sound. Daddy said it's the ships' horns so they didn't bump into each other going in and out of dock on the other side of the fence.

I spotted a patch of ginger fur. 'Come here, Peter, let me give you a cuddle. Are you imaginary? Goodness, you're heavy. You're warm. Your fur's soft. You're purring. You like being cuddled. Now, Peter, you must be good because there's going to be a street party for the Queen's Coronation and...'

Oh, there was Mummy. She was wearing her pinafore and had her cross face on. Her eyes were fierce and scary. She was coming into the garden. I was frightened. I curled into a ball. I squeezed my eyes closed. If I couldn't see her she wouldn't be there.

'Where are you, you bad girl? Just wait 'til I get hold of you. I'll teach you to hide from me!'

She was coming closer.

Don't find me, please don't find me.

'Come out of there at once. If you've got your frock dirty...'

Her hand grabbed my arm and dragged me out. The path stung my knees. She was shaking and hitting me like Peter playing with a mouse.

'Ow, ow, ow!'

She dropped me on the ground.

'Stop crying or I'll give you something to cry about.'

'I'm sorry, I'm sorry.'

Mummy picked up Peter. She was cuddling him. She was carrying him indoors.

It's hard not to cry when everything hurts. Why is hiding among the sunflowers so bad?

CHAPTER 2: GAMES OF POWER

Monday 5th May 1992, Oxford, U.K.

I wasn't aware, then, of what was happening behind closed doors – the memos, the phone calls, the games of power and control. With the benefit of hindsight, this is what I imagine took place.

In his office on the third floor, Pramod Unia studied the audit report on the Kabul office. Pramod, known simply as 'Pram', was Oxfam's Regional Manager for Pakistan and Afghanistan. Experienced in that part of Asia and as a manager, he was the boss of all who worked there in Oxfam's name.

Pram stirred sugar into his coffee and tapped the spoon on the cracked rim of his mug. He peered down at the neatly stapled pages on his desk. *'Cash in hand could not be reconciled to the books...' 'No stock control system...' 'Staff records below standard...'* The audit report was a potential disaster for the work in Afghanistan, a bomb waiting for its day to explode. He read audit recommendation five: *'Local staff require urgent training in financial and administrative procedures.'*

Pram sipped his coffee. It was essential that the books were in pristine order. The slightest hint of less than perfect accounting could end with the withdrawal of funding. The problem needed careful handling. Michael Semple had single-handedly set up the Oxfam work in Afghanistan. When the Russians withdrew in 1989, Michael went in. He negotiated budgets and funding and established a logistics office in Kabul to supply projects in remote areas. Michael had done great things, setting up programmes for rebuilding damaged roads and bridges, re-establishing agriculture and giving support to refugees returning home but the work was his baby. Outside interference would not be welcome.

Islamabad time is four hours ahead of British Summer Time. Before it got too late in the day, Pram called Islamabad.

'Michael, it's Pram in Oxford. How's things?'

'Pram, a pleasure as ever... Things are challenging but steady. What can I do for you?'

'We have a problem with the audit report from Kabul. It really comes down to our Afghan staff using a rather chaotic ledger procedure. Just thinking we can tidy up the details with one of our Oxford people who can pop over and train them up a bit.'

'Thing is Pram, if you fax over a kind of template for how you want the accounts prepared, say on a monthly basis, I think we can put that into action immediately. No need to spend extra money sending a bean counter, *eh*?'

'*Yeah*, unfortunately it's beyond that, Michael. I wish we could keep it that straightforward. I know how busy you and your staff are, which is why we need an accountant on the ground there, just for a few months. The audit report will be going to the Trustees' Audit Committee in July and we need to be seen to be taking it seriously. We don't want any hassle getting the grants through next year.'

'OK, tell you what, Pram, there're a number of good accountancy practices here and some will have branches in Kabul. I'll see if there's any assistance we can raise locally before we start packing people's bags. Could save us the expense of sending someone.'

Pram's pen moved in triangles on his jotter pad. 'OK, well, let's approach it this way. You want funding for a manager for the Kabul office. This could be our opportunity to get it. We can combine the two. Use the audit report to prove we need an office manager based in Kabul to keep things ship-shape. He or she will, of course, report to you as one of your staff.'

Michael was silent for a moment as he processed the thought. 'Yes, I can see there could be mileage in that.'

Pram smiled to himself. 'I'll send someone from Oxford as a temporary measure. When the precedent is established and the audit issue cleared, you can recruit your own person.'

'I can recruit someone here now, no problem.'

'No, Michael. Until the audit matters are resolved, it needs to be someone from Oxford to show we're taking meaningful steps. I'm sure that, between us, we'll get things sorted in Kabul so that when the Audit Committee trustees get the report we can show them we've already taken serious measures. And if we play our cards right, you'll have funding for the office manager of your choice in a few months' time. Look, it's been great talking to you, Michael. I'm sure you have things you need to do so I won't keep you. 'Bye for now.'

'OK, Pram.'

Pram pressed the phone down firmly, stared out of the window for a moment or two and then prepared a memo to his boss, the Overseas Director. The memo contained three highlighted figures from the audit report. The first was the cash delivered during the previous year, second was a total of handwritten, receipted expenditure. The third was the difference, a vast figure in U.S. dollars, rendered invisible under the muddle of the accounting. Pram wrote one sentence at the end of the page: 'Just think we need to show we are taking steps, best regards, Pram.'

It did the trick. Oxfam's Overseas Director phoned Pram the next day and told him to liaise with Michael to ensure the safe transit of one Oxford accountant to assist the bookkeepers of Kabul before the Trustees' Audit Committee meeting in July.

Monday 8th June 1992, Oxford, U.K.

It's one of those hot, muggy afternoons in Oxford when it's easy to daydream. I'm sitting at my desk in the Oxfam audit office trying to concentrate on reading audit reports from the army of bank managers, accountants, tax officials and VAT inspectors who make up the shops' volunteer audit team. It's my job to search out anything untoward and take whatever steps are necessary to get it put right.

Philip, my boss, sits at the desk to the right of mine. Six-foot plus and with fair hair, his blue eyes are deep-set as if he's been wearing his glasses for many years. I wonder whether he's worn them since he was a child. He keeps a tie hanging over the back of his chair to put on when he goes to meetings.

Philip stares out of the window for a moment then looks at me. Does he know already? Word travels fast in an office. I guess this is the moment to tell him.

'Did you see the last Vacancy Bulletin?'

Philip shakes his head.

'A secondment opportunity has come up for Kabul. You remember the audit report said the accounts are a complete shambles? Well, they're inviting applications for someone to go and sort them out and train up the local staff.'

I pause a moment. I'm strangely nervous. What's been a matter between my feelings and my mind is about to be brought out into the open.

'I've applied for it. My six years in Pakistan should be an advantage. It's the sort of work I'm already doing, so I'm hoping I've a good chance of getting it. I'd be awfully grateful if you could agree to release me for six months, if I'm appointed.'

I think Philip understands my need to be back at the heart of the action, although he has no idea of how I've grieved for the work in Pakistan. I'd loved those years. We'd worked with a hostel for twenty or so boys – who would not otherwise have been able to attend school – until Alan, my husband, developed a kidney problem. I was devastated when he became too ill to continue.

'OK. Provided they let me take on someone to cover your job while you're away, I'll release you. If you're appointed.'

'Thanks. It'll be helpful for me at the interview to tell them we've discussed it and you don't mind.'

I look down at the audit reports on my desk, trying to study them, silently savouring the familiar adrenalin rush, the buzz that makes me feel alive again.

Friday 12th June 1992, Oxford, U.K.

The interview with Pram and Pat, the lady from Personnel, is straightforward enough.

'How will you cope with the staff who only speak Dari?' asks Pram.

'Well, I was in Pakistan for six years. I got a reasonable working knowledge of Urdu and although Dari's a different language, it's closely related and has the same written script, so I hope to pick up enough to work with. Anyway, as long as there're one or two people who can speak English and interpret for me, I'm sure I can get by.'

'What would you do if your manager told you to do something that you thought was unreasonable?' asks Pat.

'Well, I'd discuss it with him, see if I could persuade him of my point of view.'

'But what if he wouldn't listen, if he couldn't understand your side of things at all?' Pram presses.

'I guess, at the end of the day, he's the boss,' I reply. 'I'd have to do as he says. Though we'd probably have a "robust discussion" first!'

I've only just returned to my desk when the phone rings.

Pat's voice says, 'We'd like you to do the secondment. Bring in your passport and we'll sort out your visas.'

CHAPTER 3: AFGHANISTAN?

Sunday 28th June 1992, Oxford, U.K.

'Afghanistan?' My husband, Alan, makes a face as if he's eating something sour. He often does that when I have a good idea.

I put a dish of roast potatoes on the table and sit down. 'That's what I said. Come on, everybody eat up before it gets cold.'

Dan takes the bowl of carrots and passes them to Mandy. Dan's my younger son, he's nineteen. He's been going out with Mandy for three years and she's one of the family now. I was dismayed when he'd left school at sixteen without even trying for his 'A' levels but he's doing OK with a succession of short-term, manual jobs.

'Mum,' says Dan, 'don't be daft. They'll cut your head off.'

'Well, we all have to depart this life sometime, dear,' I reply.

Alan reaches for the gravy. 'When?'

'In a week or two. There's some paperwork to sort out and the flights to book. I have to go to Islamabad first and travel on from there but Oxfam will deal with that. So you'll have to look after yourselves for a while – and don't pile all the work onto Mandy. I expect you each to do your share.'

Dan glances at Mandy. 'It's only for a few weeks. We'll cope.'

'*Erm*, actually, it's for six months.' Now I really have their attention.

'*Oh no*!' says Dan, 'That means I've got to clean out the hamster!'

'*Yep* and feed the cat.' Puss Puss was a stray. She kind of moved in and before we knew it she was another member of the family. 'Don't forget she needs the *Senior* cat food from Sainsbury's.'

I'm waiting for such questions as, 'Who'll iron my shirts?' and 'Who'll cook dinner?' They don't come. There's just this sort of shock while they contemplate looking after themselves for six months.

Alan and I have been together since we were teenagers. He was handsome then with his blue eyes and blond hair. His hair's grown darker over the years and now he combs the side strands over his scalp to hide the bald patch on top. He's a brilliant pianist but music work is scarce and he's keeping the wherewithal coming in with a job at a nearby factory. Alan hates the tedium of the repetitive work making moulded plastic parts to customers' orders. We can't live on my salary alone and the factory job pays well so he puts up with it.

'Why you?' he asks.

'It's my job, I have to.' I fib to forestall any emotional fireworks of the 'you care more about your work than us' variety. I do love them very much. I just need to take time out sometimes, to get away from the constant demands and come back feeling I've achieved something.

Still looking rather stunned, they mechanically pass their empty plates to me to clear away.

'*Double-0 Mum*, with her secret pen that fires people,' says Jon, my elder son.

Jon's twenty. He only gets up off the sofa to eat. Long-haired and unshaven, his main form of exercise is using the T.V. remote control. When Jon was younger, he was lively and active until the teenage *ugh* descended upon him rather heavily. He just seemed to give up on everything.

'Actually, Jon, that's not a bad idea. If I sign my letters *Double-0 Mum* you'll know it's me and that there's nothing to worry about. If I just sign *Mum* you'll know I'm in trouble and you can raise the alarm. Alan, while I'm away, don't forget to fix the gutter. Water pours down the window like the Niagara Falls every time it rains. Apple crumble for pudding. Any volunteers to make the custard? You may as well get the practice in now.'

Jon chuckles and I can't stop myself joining in. Then we're all laughing.

Thursday 2nd July 1992, Oxford, U.K.

Pat from Personnel calls me to her office to give me my visa-stamped passport and Afghanistan ID papers.

'Are you happy about everything?' she asks.

'Yes, very happy. I've been wanting to visit Kabul for some time. I got as far as the Khyber Pass when my husband and I were visiting with our sons. The Russians were in then and...'

'No, Eileen, I don't mean that. Are you happy about working with Michael Semple?'

'I'm a little nervous of meeting him. He's an Oxfam legend after all and I do admire him for what he's achieving in Afghanistan.'

Pat is leaning forward toward me in her chair. Her blue skirt and cardigan, and white blouse, remind me of my sister's school uniform.

'Thing is, Eileen, people find him difficult to get on with. They come back full of complaints about him but there's nothing we can do because Michael is the apple of Pram's eye.'

'Well, I know from my work in Pakistan that aid workers tend to be very strong people and we do sometimes clash because...'

'It's worse than that. The fact is, Michael doesn't want you. Pram is sending you against Michael's wishes. To Pram, Michael can do no wrong. Anything that doesn't go right they'll blame on you and you'll be out. I've seen it all before.'

This is awkward.

19

'I have to get back to my audit desk now, Pat. Thanks for your help with the visa and all.'

Well, what was I supposed to say? Did she seriously expect me to turn down the opportunity of a lifetime because someone's had a falling out with Michael?

I know it's crazy. I just have an innate resentment toward personnel people. Perhaps it's because their control over people's careers evokes echoes of my mother's control over me but, as I learned very early on, I don't always have to do as I'm told.

2nd June 1953, Silvertown, London, U.K.

'You sit here, behave yourself and don't show me up, or you won't be able to sit down for a week.'

'Yes, Mummy.'

I fastened the buttons on my yellow cardigan to keep out the cold. Mummy said it will rain soon. I was sitting with the other children from our street at a long table that stood in the middle of the road. It was covered in tablecloths. I liked the one with blue and white checks. There were plates piled high with egg sandwiches and jam tarts, and jugs filled with orange squash. *Yummy.*

Mummy looked different today. She wasn't wearing her wraparound pinafore or her headscarf that she used to tie at the front over her forehead. She was wearing a pretty frock with yellow flowers.

We children each had a Coronation plate, spoon and mug. I liked the picture of the Queen on the spoon. We wore homemade hats of red, white and blue paper.

'I'm going inside number 75 to watch television. Stay here, don't move, or you'll see the back of my hand, understand?'

'Yes, Mummy.'

Don't dirty your frock. Don't show me up. Don't move. Don't, don't, DON'T.

Yesterday, at Nanna and Granddad's house, we made bunting. It was fun cutting out the triangles of red, white and blue waxed paper and gluing them onto the string. Granddad had a special pot of white paste and a brush. You had to brush the glue along one side of the triangle and fold it over the string so that it glued itself to the other side of the wax paper. Mummy wasn't there. She would never let me do that.

'No,' she'd say. 'No. Scissors is sharp, you'll cut yourself.' Or, 'You think I've got nothing better to do all day than clear up after you? You'll get glue all over them clothes and you won't be no help washing 'em. No, I'll have to *and* iron them.'

Nanna didn't say that. When the glue got onto my fingers, Nanna brought me a blue towel to wipe them on. I had to wipe them a lot.

Granddad was in his chair, watching. His face was smiley. His eyes were twinkly and blue.

Nanna had white hair and she was fat! I couldn't put my arms round her waist and meet them behind her back.

We put crumpets on a long fork and toasted them in front of the coal fire and ate them with drippy butter. Nanna sat me on her lap. Mummy never did that.

Nanna smiled and spoke quietly. 'Granddad will hang the bunting over the windowsill tomorrow and whenever I look at it, I'll think, *my little Eileen made that.*'

Sitting in my place at the table in the road, I watched Bobby from next door on the opposite side. He had a blond fringe that hung down to his eyes. His paper hat was yellow with pointy tips like a crown. He licked the jam from the middle of a tart and dropped the empty pastry onto the road. If I did that, Mummy would slap my face, hard.

I went to the other side of the table and sat next to Bobby.

'My mummy's gone indoors to watch television.'

'Yes, I know. It's my house,' Bobby replied.

'What's a television?'

'Do you know what a wireless is?' Bobby asked.

'Yes. Mummy listens to it all the time.'

'Well, a television's a wireless that's got pictures.'

'I'm not allowed to do that, lick the jam out of a tart.'

'I always do.'

'Doesn't your Mummy get cross and hit you?'

'No, she doesn't mind. She lets me do it and she never hits me.'

This was confusing. Mummy always said it was bad to eat the nice bits and leave the rest. When she was my age she had to eat what she was given or go hungry. Bobby was telling me it was alright. *Bobby, Mummy, Bobby, Mummy, dip, dip, dip.*

I took a tart. I looked around to check that Mummy wasn't there. I poked out my tongue and slowly scooped out the jam. *Mmm,* that tasted good. I licked the stickiness from my lips and fingers. I checked again that Mummy wasn't watching and slid my hand under the table. Drop. The pastry plopped onto the road. Bobby was allowed to do it, why wasn't I?

Saturday 4th July 1992, Oxford, U.K.

I love my job with Oxfam. It includes lots of travel and I have packing down to a fine art. My bag is always at the ready with its well-refined checklist. I'm all set to go at a moment's notice wherever an auditor might be required to unravel a shop's spaghetti-tangled accounts or get to the bottom of a stock-control crisis. I can trace the most obscure audit trail through the confusion. I always ensure that, before I go home, everything is in immaculate order and the staff are able to continue keeping the books to Oxfam's exacting standards.

In this secondment, all my favourite things are wrapped up in one six-month posting. As Temporary Programme Support Office Manager in the Kabul office, I'm to keep the logistics flowing to the outlying projects and manage the office-based staff as well as disentangling the books and training the bookkeeper to express the accounts in a more coherent fashion. I'm as happy as a child with a new sixpence.

It doesn't take long to add the final touches. My vaccinations are up-to-date and anti-malarials in the bag. I pack my toothbrush, calculator and travel kettle.

I have one more thing to do. I visit Marks and Spencer's where I buy a dozen pairs of large white knickers. Then I go to Woolworth's and buy a dozen small wash bags with zips, the sort you put tights in when you wash them in the machine.

At home I get out my elderly sewing machine and thread it up. I stitch a wash bag into each pair of knickers to make zipped pockets that are hidden, safely and securely, inside my underwear.

Now I'm ready to set off for the Khyber Pass.

1954, Silvertown, London, U.K.

I was five years old. Mummy brushed my hair vigorously then took a handful of strands, twisted a ribbon around it and clipped the white bow onto the top of my head. She pulled me over to the light of the window and stabbed a safety pin through the corner of a handkerchief and into my cardigan pocket.

'There. That'll make sure you don't lose your hanky.'

She took a length of knicker elastic from her sewing basket, threaded it through the eye of a front door key, tied it into a loop and hung it round my neck like a necklace. We put on our coats and Mummy took me out into the street. She turned back toward the front door.

'Better make sure you know how to use it. Stand on the doorstep and open the door with the key.'

I stood on the doorstep. The lock was too high up to put the key in. Mummy took two loose bricks from the house wall and placed them on top of each other. 'Stand on them.'

I did as I was told and was able to reach the lock and open the door with the key still hanging on its elastic round my neck.

'Right. If there's no one at home when you get back, you take out them bricks and stand on 'em. Once you've opened the door, put 'em back in the wall. Understand?'

'Yes, Mummy.'

Mummy led me to school. 'When you get to this pub on the corner, look, it's got shiny brown bricks on the outside, see? You turn the corner and there's our house at the end of the road.' She turned me round to face the way we'd come.

'Now, when you come to this road, it's the entrance to the factory. Watch out for lorries coming in and out. Look both ways and don't cross 'til you're sure nothing's coming.'

Mummy took me to the school office. A lady came and took me to a classroom. I had never seen so many children in one place. Everyone sat at straight rows of desks facing the teacher's table.

'This is Eileen, she's joining your class,' said the lady.

'Eileen, this is Miss Marriott, she's your teacher.'

Miss Marriott led me to a desk. 'This is Susan, you can sit next to her.'

So many new people all at once. It was confusing.

Miss Marriott wrote the alphabet on the blackboard and we copied it into our new notebooks. We weren't allowed to talk to each other in class.

Clang! Clang!

A handbell was ringing energetically in the corridor outside. Miss Marriott led us up, up, up a dark stairwell onto the playground on the roof. The boys ran to the railings.

'Off of there!' Miss Marriott shouted. 'You know you're not allowed to climb the railings and I've a cane downstairs waiting for disobedient boys!'

The boys kicked footballs while the girls skipped or raced wooden hoops. The September sun shone down like an enormous sunflower. I felt free, alive with hope, as if I could jump onto a cloud and fly away.

Monday 6th July 1992, Oxford, U.K.

I pick up the telephone and dial my mother's number.

'I'll be away for six months. I've asked Alan to keep in touch with you and pass on my news.'

'OK, well, take care. Don't forget to send us a postcard.'

'I will if I can.'

My relationship with my mother probably appears normal to outside eyes. On the inside, not far below the surface, it's fraught with the ambivalence of an unhappy childhood. Since Dad died in 1990, two years ago now, I feel a duty toward her but my earliest memories ought to be of happy times, chasing butterflies in the garden with a laughing young mum picking me up when I fell and kissing my grazed knees better. Instead, my memories are of something quite different.

1955, Silvertown, East London, U.K.

I reached the brown-tiled pub, the landmark that told me this was my street. I turned the corner and stood still with shock. When I went to school this morning the road had been a row of houses. Now our house stood alone at the end of the street with strips of next door's wallpaper flapping from its side. I walked cautiously past the eerie footprints of the broken houses. Today, I had to be especially careful not to tread on the cracks between the paving stones. I pulled two loose bricks from the wall and stood on them to reach the lock and open the door with the key that hung around my neck.

I waited in the living room for Mummy to come home. I wanted to talk to my doll, Linda, but my toys were locked in a room upstairs. I'd have liked a drink of squash but wasn't allowed into the kitchen. I wanted to cuddle Peter, the cat, but he wasn't there.

Where are they? They must have gone away with the other houses and forgotten to take me. What shall I do? Should I go to Nanna and Granddad's house and ask them to look after me?

The sunlight through the windows was starting to fade. I jumped up at the switch to try to turn on the light. I couldn't reach it. Standing on a chair was strictly forbidden, a rule I dared not break even when Mummy wasn't there.

What's that noise? I was too frightened to go and look. Shadows started making patterns on the wallpaper like the wolf chasing Little Red Riding Hood. He was moving! He was coming out of the shapes and chasing me! I heard the door open. *Help me! The wolf's coming in!*

Daddy turned on the light and I ran into his arms.

'On your own, Girlie? Where's Mummy?'

'The houses have fallen down and I couldn't reach the light switch.'

He picked me up and sat me on his lap. His jacket was rough against my face. It smelled of the railway and sweat. Now I felt safe enough to let the tears out.

'Don't cry, Girlie. It's only the council's slum clearance. We're moving to a house near Nanna and Granddad soon.'

I heard the front door open again. Mummy came in with Kathleen in her pushchair.

'What's going on?'

'I found the child in the dark, on her own. The demolition's frightened her.'

Mummy snarled down at me. 'She's alright. I don't know why you make such a fuss of her.'

Monday 6th July 1992, Oxford, U.K.

'Passport, tickets, Kleenex tissues, book, purse, Kwell travel pills...' I make a final check of the contents of my handbag.

Alan takes the car keys from his pocket, Jon picks up his wallet and the three of us leave the house.

Alan drops off Jon and me at Heathrow airport, then goes to park the car. Dan and Mandy haven't come. Dan hates goodbyes. I understand and don't mind.

I'm wearing a cream cardigan over a white top and a calf-length, rose-print skirt that's definitely out of fashion. I have low-heeled beige sandals and I'm clutching a large, tapestry-patterned handbag with hooped cane handles. I don't bother with make-up.

Jon and I take the luggage to the check-in desk. I place my two suitcases and a box of Oxfam supplies on the conveyor scales. The reading shoots up way above the twenty-kilo mark.

'They told me I could take extra baggage. They said it would show up on your computer automatically.'

'Yes,' replies the check-in lady, 'I've got it here. Why do you need the extra?'

'I'm with Oxfam. I'm taking some stuff out.'

Airport security is less stringent than it is to become in the future and I'm not questioned about the contents of the box. I exchange my luggage for a boarding pass for the flight to Islamabad, the first stage of the journey to Afghanistan.

Jon and I find the McDonald's area and sit at a small table. Alan comes back from the car park, goes to the counter and brings us three burger meals, two colas and a large tea.

'Better eat slowly,' I say, 'there's always such a long wait at airports. They tell you to get here hours too early.'

Alan bites off a mouthful of burger. 'There's probably a lot to do behind the scenes.'

'So tell us about your new girlfriend, Jon. Bryony, isn't it? Is she pretty?'

Jon shifts uncomfortably on his seat. 'There's not much to say, Mum.'

'Alright, sweetheart, I'm only teasing you. Alan, don't forget to fix the gutter. I don't want to come back and find half the house has washed away in the deluge.'

'I said I'd fix it, didn't I?'

Eventually the flight is announced. I stand up and hook my handbag over my arm. I don't do emotional goodbyes, no clinging or crying. I peck goodbye to my husband and son and say, 'See you in six months.'

We wave to each other as I go through the gate.

Tuesday 7th July 1992, Islamabad, Pakistan

'Ladies and gentlemen, welcome to Pakistan. We are about to land at Islamabad airport. It's Tuesday 7th July, the time is 5:15 in the morning and the temperature is 29 degrees Celsius.'

The passengers give a round of applause for the pilot's successful landing, the signal for a rush to the overhead boxes and a queue for the doors. I stay in my seat. There's no point in getting up yet. The passing blur of airport buildings, buses and parked planes gradually slows to a halt.

My knees feel stiff and awkward as I follow the line of passengers along the cramped aisle. I step out onto the metal stairway and the hot, sticky air swallows me up.

Islamabad has its own sort of humid warmth, not the drenching humidity of the southern port of Karachi, nor the searing desert heat of the Sindh interior, but its own blanket of thirty-ish degrees soaked with the scent of exotic plants from the surrounding hills.

I pass through the usual checks and stand by the luggage conveyor, watching for my two black cloth suitcases. Yes, I know cloth isn't secure but it's lightweight and I have a policy of not taking with me anything I'm not prepared to lose.

A porter comes with a trolley. *'Khuli, j'naab?'* Do you want a porter?

'Haan jee.' Yes, please.

I spot my two suitcases appearing at the far end of the carousel and point them out to the porter. *'V'haan.'* Over there.

As the suitcases come closer the porter grabs the two bags and hauls them onto his trolley.

The next stop is at one of the airport's money-changing shops. I take a $50 note from my handbag and receive a small wad of Pakistani rupees. I'll change some more later when I have time to explore the money-changing shops in Islamabad's 'Blue Area' for a better rate.

Coming out of the airport in the light of the early morning, I spot a sign with the Oxfam logo on it. A young man steps forward.

'Eileen? Good morning. I'm Abbas, I work in the Oxfam office. Did you have a good trip?'

'Yes, thank you.'

The porter loads the suitcases into the car. Signs all around us announce *PORTERS CHARGE 20 RUPEES*. I pull out a one-hundred rupee note and give it to him. He nods his thanks. That should ensure I find a porter next time I come.

Abbas drops me off at the Best Accommodators Guest House. I thank him for coming out so early in the morning to meet me. He gives me a business card with the address of the Islamabad office written on it.

'Come at midday and join us for lunch.'

'OK, Abbas, I'll do that.'

It's 6:30 in the morning Islamabad time. To my body it's only 2:30 am, the middle of the night. I flop down on the bed. Despite my exhaustion, I'm too excited to sleep.

About eleven in the morning, I take a shower and dress in a pastel blue Pakistani-style *shalwar kameez,* with a long, flowing *duppatta* scarf. I've kept these clothes for the three years since I last worked in Pakistan. They've been the tangible substance of my hope to return to a place I have come to love.

The first time I put on a *shalwar* suit was in Lahore in January 1982. I felt like a clown in the shiny, pink tunic and trousers but I soon came to prefer the lightweight, cotton fabric that works so well in the heat.

I take a taxi to the office, arriving as the staff are finishing their morning's work. They look up as I enter.

'Hi! I'm Eileen Masters. Is Michael in?'

Michael's in a meeting. Abbas and the other office staff make me welcome with a glass of chilled water and a cup of tea.

I'm in plenty of time for lunch. Abbas pushes aside the papers from a desk as cardboard takeaway boxes of rice and spicy vegetables are delivered.

Now, during the years I worked in Sukkur, in the south of Pakistan, I became used to eating with a chapatti while using my right hand only (left hands are not allowed near cooked food by custom). I can break off a bite-sized piece of chapatti, curve it into a scoop and use it to pick up a tasty piece of spicy cauliflower or potato. Today, our meal involves rice and I have never got the hang of eating rice with my fingers. Yes, I know you only have to make a scoop with your middle fingers and use them to drop the rice into your mouth, assisted by your thumb but, for me, something about the procedure just doesn't work. Determined to master the process, I persevere. Pools of rice are forming on the table around my plate, on my lap and on the floor. For good manners, you are supposed only to get food on the tips of your fingers. My hand is covered up to my knuckles. The removal of the plate at the end of the meal exposes my ineptitude.

Abbas looks at me. 'What happened?' he asks.

I curl with embarrassment. 'Sorry, should have used a spoon.'

Abbas graciously changes the subject. 'Do you speak Urdu?'

'I did a short course in Urdu at Kinnaird College and had more lessons when my husband and I were working in Sukkur, though I've been back in the UK for three years and forgotten much of it now.'

'What about Punjabi?'

I only remember a few phrases but it'll take their minds off the mess of rice. So, with no regard for the strict grammar or delicate tonality of Punjabi, I play for laughs and launch into a recitation of the few lines I remember:

'How are you? I am well, thank you. What is your name? My name is Eileen. Where do you live? I live in Oxford.'

Abbas and the other staff throw their heads back in laughter. I continue my monologue.

'How old are you? I am forty-two years old. Are you married? Yes, I am married. How many boy-children do you have? I have two boy-children. How many girl-children do you have? I have no girl-children. That is all I can say, thank you very much for helping me.'

The door opens. Michael enters to the roars of laughter.

'What's going on?' he asks.

'Ha-ha!' Abbas laughs, 'Eileen is speaking Punjabi! *Ha-ha!'*

Michael looks at me a little dubiously, as well he might if he has heard my recitation. He's fluent in Urdu and Punjabi as well as Dari, the main language of Afghanistan.

I stand up. Grains of rice fall from my lap to the floor. I quickly wipe my greasy fingers on my *duppatta* scarf, pull myself up to my full five-foot-two and extend my right hand.

'I'm Eileen Masters. I'm so pleased to meet you.'

CHAPTER 4: BORED, BORED, BORED!

Tuesday 7th July 1992, By fax from Islamabad, Pakistan

Dear Alan, Jon, Dan and Mandy,

Arrived OK at 5:15 this morning. Haven't slept yet. Have drunk lots of tea instead. It's the water melon season and even at 5:15 am, it was very warm and sticky getting off the plane. Am staying at nice guest-house – 'Best Accommodators' – have a nice, clean, air-conditioned room with ensuite.

Hope to do some shopping this afternoon. A small parade of air-conditioned boutiques is calling me to buy some beautiful *shalwar kameez* suits.

Eileen/00Mum

Monday 13th July 1992, Islamabad, Pakistan

I'm bored, bored, bored! A new Suzuki pick-up is to travel with me to the Kabul office because armed gangs have stolen its previous two vehicles. I've time to kill while the Islamabad staff arrange the paperwork. I try to use the time constructively. I search the office bookshelves for books about Afghanistan. I select a Dari primer and set about learning my first words. Dari is a dialect of Persian and I already have a fair grasp of Urdu, which has one of its roots in Persian, so although just a beginner I have a bit of a head start. Still, the days are dragging and I'm longing to get on into Kabul and start my work there.

Across from the window some kind of building work is going on. Labourers in work-soiled *shalwar* suits carry bowls of bricks on their heads up a scaffold and unload them. A man wipes the dust and sweat from his face with a corner of the cloth that is wound around his head. It's dusty, back-breaking work, especially in this heat. My dad was a labourer. It must have been a bit like that for him.

1955, Royal Albert Dock, East London, U.K.

Tom Hayward stood up slowly, pressing a hand against the small of his back. He grimaced as he looked at the pile of hardcore the tipper truck was depositing in a cloud of dust.

'Should keep yer busy, Tom!' joked the driver as he crunched the Bedford in and out of reverse gear, shaking the last of the rubble loose from the lorry.

Bert Green, who formed one-eighth of Tom's platelayer gang, patted down the slack around the sleepers, evening out the spread, offering support for the heavy, iron rails. There was a barely discernible singing noise from the track.

Tom turned and peered up the line. Smoke barked from a stack. The warning whistle arrived a second later. Tom blew his whistle to warn the next gang further down the track.

For a few moments, everyone took a breather. Cyril and Blanky sparked a Woodbine apiece. Bert unwrapped the *Racing Post* and studied form. Les and Mick chatted about the dance they were going to at Greenwich that evening. Lou simply sat down, weary with age and swollen joints, whilst young Artie approached Tom like a wary puppy. The kid wanted to learn from an old hand, a foreman platelayer with three generations of steel and smoke in his soul.

'You heard the rails?'

Tom shrugged and smiled at the lad. He was keen. They all were for a month or two until the novelty of earning over £4 a week wore off and they realised this was unremitting, brutally hard graft.

'*Yeah*, you get a feel for it. Like your chairs starting to crack.'

'Chairs?'

Tom took another glance up the line to check how close the goods train was then leaned down to the track, tapping his shovel onto the heavy iron spikes, the rusted teeth that held steel clasps into the oil-stained earth.

'These grips, you call them *chairs*. It's what holds your rails fast, stops them twisting. Well, like your molars they grind a bit, then they crack one day. You can sometimes feel the difference, tap a different sound from your metal... when it's ready to break, the thing'll let you know. It'll lose its ring.'

Artie looked puzzled. The goods train clattered by in a slow concertina of bangs and thumps.

Mick shoved Artie's elbow and winked. 'I'm hoping my friend Doris will be at the dance tonight. She might lose her ring too, if she's lucky!'

The lads broke into laughter, waited for the train's soot-heavy breath to cough away towards Beckton, then picked up their shovels once more.

Sunday 12th July 1992, By fax from Islamabad, Pakistan

Dear Alan, Jon, Dan and Mandy,

So how are you all getting on? I hope you are looking after Puss Puss and Hamster and that you haven't forgotten the guttering!

I've been very glad of my travel gadgets, especially the travel kettle (yes, the adapters do fit!). The radio gets a very good reception of the BBC World Service.

There is a new TV channel, Star TV. Jon would like it. It's 90% video music of the sort he likes to watch.

I'm due to go to my next destination as soon the Suzuki is cleared, hopefully Wednesday or Thursday.

Look after each other.

Love

Eileen/00Mum

Friday 17th July 1992, Islamabad, Pakistan

Suddenly, everything is ready. The new Suzuki pick-up is registered and Zia arrives to drive me to Kabul.

'Good morning, Mrs Eileen, I am Zia.'

I nod and smile my greeting. I don't offer a handshake. Many men in Pakistan and Afghanistan feel it's not good manners to shake hands with women. I don't know whether Zia is one of them and I don't want to risk offending him.

Zia and Abbas load two metal boxes of medicines into the back of the Suzuki. Zia and I climb into the pick-up's biscuit-tin cab. Zia says a *Bismillah,* Abbas wishes us good luck and I sit back for the ninety-mile journey to our first stop, Peshawar.

Leaving Islamabad, we pick up the Grand Trunk Road, the historic sixteenth-century route that originally linked Kabul in Afghanistan with Calcutta in India. We travel northwest towards the frontier town of Peshawar. With the descent, the temperature increases. We leave behind the tree-covered hills and drive into the patchwork of greens and browns that connects the great Himalaya, now behind us, to the Khyber Mountains ahead.

The road guides us over the Indus river that gives India its name. Six hundred and twenty-five miles to the south, on the bank of the Indus, lies the city of Sukkur where my husband and I worked on an education project for boys who could not otherwise attend school. I wonder how the boys' hostel is faring and whether the school has closed for the summer holiday yet.

Reaching Peshawar, we enter a thriving city with traffic to match its status. We're surrounded by motor-rickshaws, bicycles and donkey carts all rushing along, several abreast, weaving in and out of each other with split-second timing. I shut my eyes so I can't see the nearest misses that Zia accomplishes with the precision of a circus knife-thrower. Loud music from market stalls vibrates above the sounds of people, rickshaw horns and bicycle bells. The air is scented with the crude smells of open sewage gullies and burning wood-fires.

Beyond the busy bazaar, Zia drives us into a residential area of narrow streets lined with tall, grey walls. He stops outside a high-walled entrance and sounds the horn. Large metal gates open and his cousin comes out to greet us. I don't remember his cousin's name, so I'll call him *Ahmed*.

Ahmed shows us into his house. It takes a moment for my eyes to adjust to the dimness of the room after the intensity of the sunshine outside. The front door has opened into a sort of office. There's a desk in the far corner of the room with a pile of neatly stacked books on it, and pens and pencils in a tube-like desk tidy. Behind the desk, a shelf holds a row of mottled grey-black document boxes. In the centre of the room, there's sofa and chairs around a coffee table. This is the men's reception area. No-one outside of the family passes beyond here without the permission of the man of the house.

Ahmed brings a tray with glasses of water and orange-coloured tea. 'It's bottled water,' he says to me in English.

I thank him and we sit making slightly awkward conversation, first drinking the water and then sipping the hot tea.

Ahmed takes us through to the back of the house where the family live. I see the family's sandals by the door. Zia, Ahmed and I slip off our own shoes and leave them with the others. The room is simply furnished with red rugs and sleeping mats around the sides of the room.

A young woman holding a child on her hip comes forward to greet us. I don't remember her name, so I'm calling her, *Fahima*.

'This is my wife, Fahima,' says Ahmed.

Fahima leans forward and, over the head of the child, we greet each other with a two-way kiss.

'My home is your home,' she says quietly in English.

I thank her.

We sit on the red rug. Zia and Ahmed catch up on each other's news.

Fahima brings a white tablecloth and spreads it on the floor in front of us. She brings dishes of rice, curried chicken and salad and sets them on the tablecloth. This time, I ask for a spoon. I don't want to spoil her beautiful carpet.

After the meal, the family sits to enjoy an evening's conversation. While Fahima cradles their young daughter to sleep on her lap, the talk is of earlier times under the Soviet occupation. Ahmed was imprisoned in terrible conditions. He laughs as he tells of an earthquake while he was locked in his cell and he was so afraid that he put the sanitation bucket over his head.

Perhaps something of the story was lost in Zia's translation but it doesn't sound funny to me as I contemplate the depth of fear Ahmed must have felt to cause him to do such a horrible thing. I look at Fahima and wonder how she feels about hearing the story.

It's getting late. Fahima shows me to a room and a red sleeping mat. I can hear the men up talking until late. I don't understand their conversation. I just sense an atmosphere that is fraught, uncertain.

All through the night I snatch only short moments of sleep. I look at my watch frequently, waiting for the morning.

I rise while it's still dark. Remembering Zia's caution to look poor, I slip my wristwatch and wedding ring into the pocket sewn into my underwear and that already holds a supply of U.S. dollars, my personal money for the trip. Having always been prone to travel sickness, I swallow a Kwell, a pill that normally remedies my weakness. Gathering for breakfast, we sit in a circle on the red carpet and enjoy chapatti, eggs and tea.

I feel it again when the time comes to leave, that atmosphere of sombre apprehension as Zia says goodbye to his family. At 5:15 in the morning, with the dawn call to prayer sounding over the city, we climb into the Suzuki, Zia prays a *Bismillah* and we set off for Kabul in shared, unspoken unease of what may lie ahead.

24th December 1956, East Ham, London, U.K.

I already have two sisters now, Kathleen and Mary, and it was a surprise when Nanna Hayward came to the house. Mum went upstairs and Nanna stayed downstairs with us. I started to go up to the bathroom. Nan called me down.

'Don't go up there, dear, Mum's tired. She's sleeping. I'll look after you 'till she's better.'

'But I want to go to the bathroom.'

'*Oh, er*... let me check.'

Nanna stood on the second stair up and peered up toward the bathroom door.

'Alright dear, you can go up but be quick and come straight down again.'

This was odd. Didn't Nanna realise I was seven now and I could go to the bathroom by myself whenever I wanted? Nanna sat in Mum's chair. She'd brought a set of wooden bricks with her, all in pretty, bright colours. Kathleen, she was four, built them up into a tower. Mary, she was two, knocked them over. Nanna laughed.

'Would you like a cup of tea, Nanna?' I asked. Mum always offered tea to visitors and if she wasn't there, I supposed it would be my job to do it, being the eldest daughter.

'No thank you, dear. I expect we'll need one for your mum soon.'

Something felt wrong. Mum didn't go to bed in the middle of the day. She'd lie on the sofa if she had one of her heads and Nanna, why was Nanna here looking after us? She seemed sort of tense, uneasy. I could feel it. Why would mum need a cup of tea soon? *I don't understand, what's going on?*

Through the doorway I saw a lady come half-way down the stairs. I didn't know she'd been up there. Nanna jumped up with a worried look on her face.

'Everything alright, Nurse?'

I rushed out behind Nanna, curious to know what was happening.

The nurse leaned over the banister. 'You've got a present from Father Christmas, a baby sister, Christine. Two teas, please, Mrs Hayward, one with plenty of sugar in it.'

The nurse disappeared into Mum and Dad's bedroom.

Oh, no. Not another sister I'll be expected to share my toys with.

Friday 17 July 1992, Oxford, U.K.

Hi, Mum,

Dad says you will be going to Peshawar today.

Peshawar! Do you remember our holiday there with the Burrows family? That's where I first started to learn to read Urdu script. I remember spelling out 'Coca Cola' on the advertising hoardings.

We went swimming every day. Dan and I would go with you, Jean Burrows and her kids to the morning ladies' session at a local private club and we'd swim for an hour or so then stop for a 'bottle', usually Sprite because the Sprite bottles had more drink in them than the 7-Up bottles and we were going through a lemonade phase at the time.

It was hot! Dan and I slept on the roof under mosquito netting but the wretched things just ended up trapped under the net and we'd still get eaten alive. The only relief at that time was the utterly ineffective Calamine lotion. We'd be wandering around with stupid pink splotches all over ourselves.

When we got back from the morning swim, the cook would have made a hot curry for lunch that we'd utterly devour. I remember he was a brilliant cook and in the heat, the hot curries were a godsend. I also remember raiding the fridge quite a bit because he made a mean custard tart too.

Jumping out of the van I got a deep cut on my ankle (still got the scar) when we were on our way back from the Khyber Pass – that night I was asleep on my *charpai,* string bed, and I woke up with searing pain in the cut. It was dark so I couldn't see what was going on. There was a little room on the roof with a light and a small adjoining loo. When I switched on the light I saw that my cut was full of ants. Not only that but there was a trail of ants going across the roof, up one of the legs of my *charpai* and into my cut ankle. I washed the ants out and spent the rest of the night trying to sleep with my right leg over my left knee... if you see what I mean. The next day I was too worried to mention it to Jean in case she wanted to give me some kind of injection! In the end she put butterfly stitches over it.

I've never forgotten the view from the Mujahedeen positions of the road winding through the pass and being told that the patch of green on the other side was Afghanistan. I also remember that Dan and I were invited into the back of one of the many local gun shops where skilled craftsmen would make thousands of knock-off AK-47s to sell to the local tribesmen. They offered Dan and me the chance to try some handguns. At 10 or 11 years old it was about time that we were properly armed!

Anyway, I'm glad to know you're having fun!
Jon.

CHAPTER 5: THE FIRST DAY IS THE WORST

Sunday 19th July 1992, Kabul, Afghanistan

'Mrs Eileen, Mrs Eileen, please come, please come quickly.'

It's Sunday 19th July 1992 and my first day as Temporary Programme Support Office Manager in Kabul. It's 6:45 in the morning, an hour before the working day starts and someone is frantically banging on my bedroom door. I'm never fully functional before my first cup of tea in the mornings. I ignore it for a moment hoping some other solution will be found.

'Oh, Mrs Eileen, it's me, Nafisa, please hurry!'

I throw a *duppatta* scarf over my crumpled *shalwar kameez* that I slept in last night because I didn't want to be embarrassed if they had to dig me out from under the rubble this morning. I open the door. I see an Afghan woman, probably in her twenties, her body tense with fear.

'They want to open the boxes, come quickly.'

Over the years, I've found that the first day in any job is always difficult. I can see today is not going to be any different. Nafisa leads me to the main office. I recognise some of the gang who checked our pick-up last night.

'You can kill me if you want but don't take the medicines!' Nafisa is pleading.

I admire her loyalty but this seems somewhat extreme to me. I attempt some calming words in English, hoping that Nafisa will interpret them into Dari.

'There are only medicines and dressings in the boxes ready to be sent to one of our other offices for use among the wounded. You can open them if you want but they are for the benefit of your people.'

Nafisa's agitation suggests that the calming effect is not getting through in translation.

Zia arrives. He smiles and greets everyone politely, with a friendly handshake for each of the intruders. Zia introduces me to the gunmen. He explains that I arrived yesterday.

'This is her home. She is here to help us. You should show her respect.'

The intruders shift uncomfortably on their feet and look down at the floor.

Zia's infectious calmness works its magic again. Satisfied that there are no guns, only medicines and a crazy foreign woman, the gunmen leave with handshakes for Zia and polite nods to me.

'Zia is right, Mrs Eileen,' Nafisa says, after the intruders have left. 'In our culture it is a very bad thing to intrude into someone's home.'

'They said they did not know you were here,' says Zia. 'They said that now they know, they will not disturb you again and they will protect you and stop anyone else from intruding.'

I'm not sure this is the kind of protection I want.

There's something else on my mind now, something that doesn't feel right. Yesterday, we were stopped three times, then the intruders this morning. They were all suspicious about the boxes. Why are Zia and Nafisa so anxious about opening a couple of medical chests? Why don't they simply open the boxes and show everyone that there are only medical supplies inside them?

After stress-relieving cups of sweet-spiced tea all round I call Zia and Nafisa aside.

'What's in those boxes?'

They look at each other.

'Come on, Nafisa, there's no need to look at Zia, just tell me, please.'

'Twenty thousand U.S. dollars,' Nafisa replies.

Zia explains that *medicine* is the code-word for cash and disguising it as medicines is the only way to transport it safely. Others have worked out that our vehicles are covertly carrying something across the country. They have speculated as to what it may be and decided that we are gun-running.

I try to ignore the shiver that trickles down my spine.

Zia goes to the codan radio, 'Alpha India, Alpha India, this is Juliet Kilo,' he repeats until the radio scratches and a voice answers.

'Good morning, Juliet Kilo, this Alpha India. Over.'

'Please telephone our Oxfam office in Islamabad and give them the message that our visitor has arrived. Over.'

'I copy you, Juliet Kilo, we will do that for you. What is the weather in your location? Over.'

'Weather is very noisy. Over.'

After the call, Zia explains to me that the Mujahedeen have stolen numerous radios. We have to assume they are listening and mustn't give away any security information, or give them any clues as to where they might find a foreigner to abduct, or an office to raid. He says he will go to the United Nations (U.N.) building to notify them of my arrival. It's safer that way.

'Before you go, Zia, I would like you and Nafisa to call me *Eileen*, just *Eileen*, without *Mrs*.'

Zia frowns. 'No, Mrs Eileen. It is not possible. If anyone hears me, they will think I show no respect.'

Nafisa looks thoughtful. 'What do people call you in England?'

'They just say, '*Eileen*'.

'Not *Mrs*?'

'*Mrs* is for strangers. Friends and family say, *Eileen*'.

Nafisa ponders this thought for a moment then raises her head decisively.

'While you are here, we are your family. I will call you *Eileen*.'

With a glance of disapproval at Nafisa and apparently oblivious to the explosive thumps, bangs and thuds going on outside, Zia leaves to go to the U.N. office. To him, at the time of his birth, Allah decided when and how he would die. So what has he to fear?

An older man comes in. I recognise his face from last night. Over his green *shalwar* suit, he's wearing a pinafore with blue and white flowers printed on it. He's short and thin. His dark hair and moustache are beginning to grey. Nafisa interprets for me.

'Eileen, this is Musa. He is *chowkidar* and also the cook. He is saying he met you last night when you arrived. He made tea for you and you must have liked it too much because you drank four glasses.'

We all laugh.

'He says he speaks a little English and some French because he was once a cook in a hotel in France, in the Champs-Elysées.'

Nafisa sends Musa for more tea and she and I sit down together.

'Do you enjoy your work here?' I ask.

'I am too much happy here. It's not for need of the money. I have father and brothers. My father says I do not need to work. I tell him it makes me very happy. When I give him my salaries, he asks me what I need. I tell him I need clothes, shoes and make-up for work and he gives me everything, everything!'

I blow on the top of my glass to cool the scalding tea and take a cautious sip. 'That sounds like a good arrangement.'

Nafisa leans toward me as if she's telling me some great secret.

'Is it true that in England women don't have to marry?'

44

'Yes, it's true.'

'Is it also true that a woman can live alone?'

'Yes, my three sisters all live alone in their own houses.'

'They don't have to marry?'

'No, they can marry or not, as they wish.'

'I wish I could stay unmarried and live alone.' Nafisa sighs with the weary realisation that she will probably never achieve this simple ambition.

'You are married, Eileen?'

'Yes. I married in 1970.'

'What is your husband's name?'

'Alan.'

'Love marriage or arranged?'

'It was a love marriage.'

'Your parents let you choose?'

'Yes. That's our custom.'

Nafisa's long, black eyelashes look down into her lap. 'My parents will choose a cousin for me and I will marry him. You know, I don't want to marry, ever, but in Afghanistan a woman carries the honour of her family and I love my family too much. I cannot dishonour them.'

Nafisa tells me she has brothers and sisters but her eldest brother died. He was in the Afghan Air Force when the Russians took over. He was ordered to bomb Panjshir. He refused, saying he would not kill his own people. The Russians shot him through the head. His Afghan colleagues brought his body home.

'Eileen, I was so distressed. I was crazy with the death of my dear brother.'

Nafisa shows me around the bungalow that serves as an office for Oxfam and as my accommodation. It smells of furniture polish and is spotlessly clean. The bungalow is built around a central square under a clear dome that lets the light in through the roof. Here, a sofa and two armchairs sit on the red carpet and between them a coffee table. One side of the square is the entrance. A number of interconnected rooms surround the other three sides. The bungalow was built as a home, so it is designed to allow the women to move from room to room out of sight while the men of the house receive visitors in the central square.

'This is Zia's office connecting to yours and this is the office I share with Ehsan. He's Zia's assistant.'

On the third side of the square is the kitchen, a dark room smelling of cylinder gas and kerosene.

'Eileen, there are three bathrooms and a problem. I am too much afraid to go to the bathroom because the men see me go to the door. Especially the guards, Samimi and Babur, they grin and wink at me if they see me. I usually go to this one, by the kitchen, because I can walk outside and come in through the kitchen and no-one sees me, but sometimes Zia or Ehsan is in there and I am too much embarrassed.'

We go to my office and find three pieces of paper. I slowly write in large Farsi script. I could have asked Nafisa to write it but I am determined to try for myself. The first piece of paper says *Private*. We sellotape it onto the door of the bathroom next to my bedroom. It has a Western-style toilet and a bath. This does not appeal to Afghan cultural taste, whereas it does appeal to mine and I am requisitioning this bathroom so that I can keep my toiletries in there. It's part of my 'nesting' process, I suppose.

On the second paper I write *Zenaana*, Ladies only. We sellotape that onto the door of the bathroom by the kitchen. On the third piece I write *Mardaana*, men only, and we stick it onto the door of the third bathroom. Nafisa smiles and clasps her hands together in joy.

Won't it be nice if all the problems of the Kabul office are this easy to solve?

Nafisa giggles. 'That is old-fashioned writing!'

'But everyone will be able to read it?'

'Yes, they can read it. Thank you.'

'Let's go outside, I'd like to see the garden.'

'Oh, no, Eileen. We are next to the Ministry of the Interior. It is impossible for women to go in the garden.'

I look out of the window at the building next door. Armed men are sitting on its second-floor balcony watching out over the streets and overlooking our grounds.

'If we go outside, they will think bad thoughts and maybe do evil things and it will be our fault, Eileen, for letting them see us. Come on, I will show you the accounts books.'

Zia returns. 'UN offices are closed. All are in their bunkers. I could not inform them. I will go again tomorrow.'

'OK, thanks for trying,' I reply.

'You should write a letter of condolence from the Oxfam to Halo Trust,' Zia continues. 'Two days ago, two of their men were clearing mines. They were blown up. One was trapped. Other escaped but he went back to rescue friend. One is dead, other is dying. Red Cross has tried to fly him out but airport is under too many rockets.'

'OK. I'll do that today.'

Outside, an explosion interrupts the rolling, thunderous booms.

Nafisa is looking agitated. 'I am very sorry. I must go home now. My father did not want me to come today because of the rockets. I told him you were coming and I must be here. He will worry too much if I do not return quickly.'

Zia hasn't said anything about his family but I sense that he's anxious, too.

'OK, both of you go to your families. Thank you for coming in despite the rockets today.'

They drive away in the Suzuki.

I sit down on a chair in the office. I'm not feeling well. Although I enjoy travelling, I've never been a good traveller. Yesterday's journey has left me feeling queasy and off-balance, as if my head is still bouncing along the road.

Musa comes in with a glass of tea on a tray. 'Mrs Eileen, breakfast?' he asks.

'*Nay, ta-shukur.*' No, thankyou.

'Dinner? English special?'

I hesitate. I'm not sure I'll want dinner.

'Mrs Eileen, yesterday no supper. Today no breakfast. Eat is must. English dinner, special.'

I suppose he's right. I ought to eat something. '*Ta-shukur, Musa, khoob ast.*' Thank you, Musa, that's lovely.

Outside the thumps, thuds and explosions continue. I lie on my bed. Lying down in the middle of the day feels lazy. I get up and walk around the offices. Like Alice in Wonderland, I find a key on my desk. I wander around trying it in various doors until it turns in a cupboard keyhole. It's the stationery cupboard, filled with assorted books, notepads and computer printer paper. I close the door, lock it and return the key to its place.

I sit at the computer and turn it on. It doesn't take long to come to life. It seems to have the usual 1992 applications, *Word Perfect* for letters and documents, *QuattroPro* for numbers. I peruse the computer files. There are a few items of correspondence. Here's an interesting file. Someone has started putting the cash books onto a spreadsheet, the computer equivalent of a large sheet of paper with a grid for organising numbers.

I'm very tired when Musa comes and stands in the doorway. He points with his chin to the dining room.

I understand. I go and take my seat at the dining table, neatly set with a plate, knife and fork and a selection of serving spoons.

Musa reappears with a jug of water and a glass. 'Water is boil,' he explains, placing them in the centre of the table.

With a flourish, he shakes open a folded napkin and gives it to me. I place it on my lap and smile my thanks.

He brings in a dish of hot rice with flaked chicken and almonds, then stands watching me, smiling. The meal tastes good and I realise for the first time that I have an appetite. With each spoonful I eat, Musa nods with the satisfaction of seeing me enjoy the meal he has prepared. I think he feels the same as I do when my family enjoy the food I've prepared for them.

I put my spoon and fork down on my plate and Musa whisks them away to the kitchen. A few moments later, he returns with another plate, spoon and fork and places them in front of me. He brings a dish of melon pieces, grapes and sliced apple. His smile grows even wider as I take a portion. Then he brings a glass of tea.

I want to say it was a perfect meal and I've enjoyed it very much but neither my Dari nor Musa's English includes that much vocabulary. I simply say, *'Ta-shukur. Bissior khoob ast.'* Thank you. It is too many beautiful.

It's only eight-thirty in the evening but I can't stay awake any longer. My bedtime lullaby is the cacophony of artillery and rocket fire crashing down outside. I drift into sleep remembering another time of conflict, so long ago, and now so very far away.

1957, East Ham, London, U.K.

'John Salter! What are you looking for in your pocket that is more important than doing your arithmetic?'

'Nothing, Miss.'

I always wanted to laugh when Mrs Jessop did that, knowing what someone was doing behind her back and spinning round to catch them out. I squeezed my lips together to stop a giggle getting out.

Mrs Jessop had written sums on the blackboard and was walking around the rows of desks, inspecting each of our notebooks. She was so tall and thin. Her grey hair was tucked up with hairpins at the back of her head. What would happen if someone crept up behind her, really quietly, and took a hairpin out? Would all her hair fall down?

I was good at sums, like that one there, six fours, easy, twenty-four. I liked the way sums were always the same. Six threes were always eighteen, secure, unchanging eighteen. Sums were my friends, blotting out what was happening at home, like a curtain that shuts the scary darkness outside.

'Eileen Hayward, what is that mark on your arm?'

Everyone was looking at me. I tugged the sleeve of my cardigan down.

'Nothing, Miss. I grazed it.'

Mum's words were filling up my head. 'Nobody will believe you, they'll just think what a naughty little girl you are for telling lies and punish you worse.'

Mrs Jessop looked down at me with her bird eyes that saw everything. She took hold of my arm and pulled up my cardigan sleeve.

'How did you get that?'

'I... I fell against a wall, Miss'

'What wall? Where? No wall did that.'

'I might have... I think I dropped something on it, Miss... my hairbrush.'

Stifled giggles came from the other children.

Mrs Jessop was getting angry. 'No. Dropping a brick might do that, not a hairbrush. You're lying to me, Eileen Hayward, and we do not have liars in this class, do we?'

My face was burning with embarrassment. 'No, Miss.'

I desperately wanted to say, 'Miss, it was my mum, I spilled milk on my frock and she punched my arm,' but the words were locked up in my head and wouldn't come out and Mrs Jessop was angry and getting ready to punish me worse for telling lies and I didn't know what to say.

Mrs Jessop looked around the classroom. Everyone was watching, waiting for me to get a dose of the slipper in front of them all. I was struggling not to cry.

'Hmm, if there's any fighting going on at break-time, I shall find out about it and someone will be receiving the cane. We do not tolerate bullies, especially those who pick on the smallest girls. Do I make myself clear, class?'

'Yes, Miss,' voices chanted around me.

I put my head down on the desk with my hands over my face so no one would see my tears.

CHAPTER 6: *BISSIOR ROCKET!* (Too many rockets!)

Monday 20th July 1992, Kabul, Afghanistan

As I wake up, the first thing I notice is that I'm still alive. The second thing is that the noises outside are even more intense than when I went to sleep last night.

Musa brings a tray with a glass of tea, a hot naan bread and scrambled egg and puts it on the small table in my room. A particularly loud boom rattles the windows and he looks up.

'Bissior rocket!' Too many rockets, he says.

I nod in agreement. *'Bissior rocket,'* I repeat.

After breakfast, Zia arrives. 'I cannot stay, I must go back to my family. I came to see you are OK.'

'Yes, I'm fine. Just one thing before you go, please show me where the accounts files are kept?'

Zia unlocks a cupboard containing an assortment of large black lever files and smaller ring binders. They are stuffed with oversized papers that have gone brown at the edges.

'You keep all the accounts on paper, not the computer?'

'Yes. Before you came, two computers were stolen by Mujahedeen, so now everything is in books.'

Musa is hovering in the doorway. He speaks to Zia.

'Musa says he needs to go home. He has been here all night because of his *chowkidar* duties and he needs to go now to see his family is OK. He has left you lunch, soup and naan, in kitchen. He will return in time to prepare evening meal.'

'OK. Please tell him to give my regards to his family and I hope they are all safe and well.'

'And now...'

'Yes, Zia, you need to go. I understand, but first, please open the safe for me before you leave, I need to count the money.'

I'm keeping Zia when he needs to be away but I must get this task done if I'm to do anything useful today.

With Musa still at the door hoping for a lift home, Zia and I count the money. We agree the amount, write it into the cash book with today's date and we both sign it. We return the money to the safe. I pick up some files and take them to my desk.

Musa speaks to Zia.

'Musa says you should sit underneath desk. It will be safer.'

I walk with them to the door. 'And you should go by Suzuki. That will be safer for you.'

Watching the Suzuki drive out through the gates, I stand in the doorway. A plane flies overhead. From its belly flashes a flurry of red flares. I want to run away. Where to? Anywhere else will be just as bad. I can't look. I go inside and shut the door.

So here I am, alone. From my hiding place underneath the desk, sheltered, theoretically at least, from the war raging outside, I look for comfort in something familiar, the accounts.

I scan through the pile of papers, books and files. There's nothing before 30th April 1992. They must have disappeared in one of the lootings.

So far, no-one has been able to agree the actual cash in the safe to the cash book balance. I notice that there are various different styles of handwriting in the cash book. *Ah*, more than one person is writing up the book, a recipe for bookkeeping disaster.

I start the books afresh with a column in the cash book for a running total, starting with today's actual amount. This will set Nafisa on the straight and narrow and, from today, what the book says we have will be here in countable cash. That's the easy bit done.

Now I have to unravel what went wrong before today. I trace the trail from the receipt of dollars from Oxford into the

Kabul bank account through to the cash expenditure in Afghan currency. I find a number of incoming monies have been written in twice. No, wait a minute. This one's been entered three times! So the money's not missing after all, it's just too many hands not knowing what the previous hands did.

This is crazy. I'm sitting underneath a desk, calmly checking the accounts while hell rages outside. It's a strange way to settle into a new assignment even though settling in is something at which I've had a fair bit of practice.

It doesn't seem long ago that Alan and I were settling in to our work at the boys' hostel in Sukkur in the searing heat of Sindh in southern Pakistan.

April 1986, Sukkur, Sindh, Pakistan

It was a relief to step out of the scorching sun, through the curtain into the darker, cooler, room. Thirty-five boys rose in unison to their feet.

'Good morning, boys,' said the boarding master, Nazir Alum.

'Good morning, Sir,' chorused the boys.

Nazir led my husband, Alan, and me to the table placed cross-ways at the head of the boys' long, wooden table. As we took our seats, all thirty-five boys sat down in a single movement like a well-trained choir.

The boys waited silently and patiently. The combined smell of spicy food and sweating bodies grew stronger as Nazir gave a lengthy speech of welcome in Urdu.

Lunch was getting late. All the boys were sitting upright on the long wooden benches at the tables.

'Names!' commanded Nazir.

Each boy in turn stood smartly to attention, said his name, which area he was from, his grade in school, and then sat down.

With the mouth-watering aroma of curry torturing our appetites and presumably those of the boys too, Nazir prayed a long grace that reviewed the main points of his speech of welcome. It was like living a scene from *Oliver Twist*, except that the boys looked happy and well-fed.

Two of the bigger boys brought in a huge cauldron of food and at another command from the boarding master, one of the boys took our plates, filled each with generous portion of mutton curry and placed a piping-hot chapatti on the side.

In complete silence, the hostel boys took their plates to the cauldron for their curry and chapattis. The boys ranged in age from five to fifteen years. All were from backgrounds that meant they would not be able to attend school where they lived.

I watched the boys carefully. I was concerned in case they were unhappy in this almost military environment. I was relieved to see that they were enjoying tucking into their lunch, most going back for second and even third helpings.

As the boys finished their meal, they silently took their dishes to the kitchen and returned to their seats.

'Boys, stand!' commanded Nazir. 'Boys, dismiss!'

With well-rehearsed precision, the boys marched out of the dining room.

Alan and I were left alone with Nazir and cups of sweet, milky tea.

'You see, Mr and Mrs Alan, this building was once the palace. It was built by General Napier when British first conquered Sindh. He never came and building was abandoned because of fierce climate. Over years it has been used as Hindu temple and as part of *Zenaana*, women's, hospital across the road.'

He explained that large parts of the building had become unusable, especially where the roof had fallen in over the original palace rooms. The hostel boys, he said, were strictly forbidden to enter the palace rooms because of the danger from the unstable roof.

Our apartment was in better condition. The building, made of mud and straw, was always a few degrees cooler inside than out, for which we were very grateful.

Our first job was to get the place cleaned up. With Sindh dust blowing into the building continuously and the apartment not having been used for nearly three years, cleaning up was going to be a major operation. Various species of ants were swarming between the floor's flagstones amid the layers of amber, desert dust.

'We'll have a floor-washing-and-ice-cream party!' Alan said.

Twenty or so giggling hostel boys aged from 5 to 15 arrived and gathered in the garden, keen and eager to help. Alan stood by the ground water-tank. This was the tank into which our ration of water came once a day. It was a simple technology. We used an electric pump, of the sort that's sometimes used in caravans, to pump the water from the ground tank up to the roof tank and gravity brought the water down to the taps.

'Come and fill your buckets from the ground tank,' called Alan, holding a hosepipe he'd fixed up to supplement the buckets.

'Sir, can I use the hosepipe?'

'No, me, Sir, let me have it!'

'Thank you, boys. Sunil, you can have it first, then Ghulaam.'

Alan handed the wet hose to Sunil. A moment later there was a shriek from a soaked Ghulaam.

'The water goes on the floor, Sunil.'

'Sorry, Sir, I missed.'

'Ghulaam, use the broom to sweep the water out of that hole under the door.'

'Yes, Sir.'

The two smallest boys, Yousef and Nataani, came in carrying a bucket between them. Taking careful aim, they threw the water over Ghulaam and ran away as Ghulaam chased them with his broom.

Excited voices sounded outside.

'Like this, come on, over the side, down you go!'

Alan and I rushed out into the garden. One of the boys had dropped his bucket into the ground water tank. The other lads had tied the hosepipe round Nataani's waist and were lowering him into the tank to retrieve it.

'Bus! Bus!', Stop! Stop! we both shouted as little Nataani began making his descent into the water.

Behind us, a cheer went up from the boys now gathered outside to watch this scene and dry themselves in the hot sunshine. The ice-cream man had arrived at the gate, signalling the end of a soggy job well done.

Monday 20th July 1992, Kabul, Afghanistan

I'm starting to feel the lack of exercise. I remember Nafisa's warning not to go into the garden and anyway, I don't want to be outside under this particular sort of storm. I go to my room and take my skipping rope out of my suitcase.

I skip to the rhythmic rhyme I'd learned in the school playground.

> *'Cobbler, cobbler, mend my shoe*
> *Get it done by half past two.*
> *Half past two is much too late*
> *Get it done by half past eight.'*

It's seven in the evening now and dark outside. Musa hasn't returned. Is he lying wounded or dead under the ruins of his house? No, I must switch off the pictures in my mind. He's probably OK, I mustn't assume the worst.

57

I find some 'English special' left over in the fridge from yesterday and warm it up for my supper. It's just as appetising today as it was when Musa made it yesterday.

It's nine in the evening and I'm getting ready to go to bed. There's an unexpected silence. The onslaught has stopped. At last.

Tuesday 21st July 1992, Kabul Afghanistan

I'm only just up and dressed when there's a knock on my door. I open it and Musa brings in a breakfast tray. He's not looking his usual smiling self.

'Mrs Eileen, dinner. Problem. *Bissior rocket!*'

I guess he is trying to explaining his non-return last night.

I smile and nod. 'English special, from the fridge.'

Zia comes in through the kitchen with Nafisa and another man and woman.

'Mrs Eileen, this is Ehsan, he is clerk and assists me, he can also drive. This is Gulshad, she cleans and helps Musa in kitchen.'

Nafisa is wringing her hands. 'Eileen, I was too much worried about you yesterday. I said to my father I must come in case you need me and see that you are OK. He forbade me to leave the house because of the rockets.'

Zia speaks. 'Musa says he is very sorry he could not return to cook dinner and for his *chowkidar* duties last night. Rockets were too many and his family insisted he stay with them. He says he was very worry about you.'

'Well, please assure him that I understand and I'm fine and I don't want anyone taking risks for me. It's nice having you all looking after me but I can look after myself too, you know.'

Ehsan, Zia's assistant and Gulshad, the lady who does the cleaning are equally apologetic for their absences.

I tell them how pleased I am to meet them. Nafisa takes the opportunity to tell them I have allocated bathrooms. Gulshad smiles and nods. The men look puzzled but don't protest.

Zia, Ehsan and Nafisa go to their desks, Musa goes to the kitchen and Gulshad starts polishing the coffee table.

Tuesday 21 July 1992, Kabul, Afghanistan

Hello everyone,

On Thursday, I got up to Murree just for a very quick visit and met some of the school staff who taught Jon and Dan. Behind the Sandes boarding block they now have a block of flats for the single teachers. The whole area is a complete mess as they are doing so much building work there.

On Friday I went to Peshawar. I stayed overnight with an Afghan family then we left at 5:15 on Saturday morning for Kabul. Altogether the journey took nearly 16 hours and we arrived at 8:15 pm local time. The road was very bad with the debris of war everywhere. In an area controlled by extremists some warning shots were fired over us. I didn't understand what it was about until the person driving me, Zia, said, 'Your face hide.' It wasn't enough that I was wearing a *chador* shawl and my head was covered. When I pulled my *chador* up over my face they stopped firing.

Although it was quiet when we first arrived in Kabul, at 2 in the morning (Sunday) I was woken by the sound of rocket fire. Although Sunday is a working day, many of the staff were unable to get into work because of the rocket fire. Those who did were anxious about their families and left early.

The battle continued through Sunday night and Monday and finally ceased at 9 pm on Monday. I was still feeling quite unwell from the journey on both Sunday and Monday. (I am a lot better today.) On Sunday I felt particularly bad with the combination of the long and difficult journey plus one and a half nights without sleep. At about 8:30 pm I piled all my spare bedding up on the windowsill and plugged in the nightlight that always travels with me. It's an indication of how tired I was that I slept through the night despite the continuing sound of rocket attacks. From what people have told me, I was the only one in Kabul who did sleep that night!

Conditions are much better since the fighting stopped on Monday evening.

The office is in a large bungalow and if it were not for the conflict it would be very pleasant. There is a good-sized garden in which I would like to see vegetables growing. There are three bathrooms of which I have requisitioned one for my private use so I can leave my stuff in there and don't have to remember to take my soap with me in the mornings! At the request of the female staff, the other two are now designated *Ladies* and *Gents*. As well as the offices, there are my bedroom, two guest rooms and quarters for the guards and *chowkidar*.

The *chowkidar* is quite a character. He is also the cook. He used to work in Paris on the Champs-Elysées. He wears a white pinafore with blue flowers printed on it and is most particular how things should be done. He speaks a little English and is always anxious to help. He was concerned that I wasn't eating on Sunday when I felt so ill and tried to make an English meal. It consisted of rice with grated carrot and sultanas followed by melon.

We have radio contact with the U.N. and other agencies in Afghanistan. We also have contact with the U.N. office in Islamabad and they pass on our messages by telephone to Michael. The reverse process gets messages from Michael to us.

Anyway, I hope you are all taking care of each other.

Love to all

Eileen/00Mum

Tuesday 21st July 1992, Kabul, Afghanistan

I sit on the sofa and signal to Gulshad to join me. I hold up one hand. Pointing to each of my fingers in turn, I say,

'English – one, two, three, four, five. Dari?'

Gulshad understands. *'Yaak, doe, say, chaa, paanj,'* she says slowly.

I try to repeat the words. *Yaak, doe* and *chaa*, one, two and four, are easy to remember because they are almost the same as Urdu. *Paanj*, five, is easy because it's the same in Punjabi. *Say*, three, reminds me of *tray*, the word for 'three' in the Pahari mountain dialect I've heard spoken in the Murree hills. So I'm picking it up quite quickly even if I'm cheating slightly as I go.

The lesson continues until I've mastered the numbers one to ten.

January 1982, Kinnaird College, Lahore, Pakistan

My first Urdu lessons were at Kinnaird College, Lahore. From the bungalow in which we were staying, it was a crisp, ten-minute walk in the early morning chill.

My teacher, Mr Javeed, was keen on role-play.

'I am the shopkeeper. You want to buy some apples. What do you say?'

'Mihabaani kar-kay, ek kilo seb.' A kilo of apples, please.

'No. First you must greet me.'

'Asalam-alaikum. Mihabaani kar-kay, ek kilo seb.' Greetings. A kilo of apples please.

'No. You must greet me and then ask after my health.'

'Asalam-alaikum. Apka kya haal hai' How are you?

'I am well, and you?'

'I am well, thank you. A kilo of apples, please.'

'No! first you must ask after my family. Then you can ask for apples.'

Alan looked after Jon and Dan in the mornings while I was at my class. On my return, I took over care of the boys while

Alan went for his lesson. Even in winter, the Lahore sun shone while Jon and Dan played in the grassy grounds. It was exciting to visit the magical places we had read of but never seen before – Anarkali Bazaar, the Shalimar Gardens and 'Kim's gun' made famous by the Kipling novel and still standing outside the Lahore Museum.

One day, I came to my lesson as usual. Mr Javeed seemed in a restless mood. He peered out of the window then went to the door and looked outside. He returned and sat on his chair opposite mine. These chairs were the only two pieces of furniture in the room apart from a small table by the window on which stood a glass and a jug of water, the top neatly covered with a lace handkerchief.

Mr Javeed leaned forward.

'There were two dogs, an Indian dog on his way to Pakistan and a Pakistani dog on his way to India. They met at the border.

'The Pakistani dog asked the Indian dog, "Why you are coming to Pakistan?"

'The Indian dog replied, "Because I'm hungry. I've heard there is food in Pakistan. I've come to eat. Why are you going to India? Is there not enough food in Pakistan?"

'The Pakistani dog answered, "There's plenty of food in Pakistan."

'The Indian dog didn't understand. "So why are you going to India?"

'The Pakistani dog looked around. Seeing there was nobody to overhear him, he whispered, "Because I'm not allowed to bark!"

'And that, Eileen, is about the previous regime and you must remember, while we are under the martial law of General Zia Al Haq, every joke is about the previous regime.'

CHAPTER 7: SHEER INSANITY!

Wednesday 22nd July 1992, Kabul, Afghanistan

'We need to start a radio log to record all our calls, in and out. Then if there are any problems or misunderstandings, we'll be able to look at it and see what was said.'

'Yes, Eileen.' Nafisa replies. 'When I worked for W.H.O., that's the World Health Organisation, do you know it? We had to write down every call and the calls we tried to make but couldn't get an answer.'

Zia brings a hardcover book from the stationery cupboard and carefully rules some vertical lines down the first few pages.

'This column is for date,' he says, 'this column for name of person calling.'

'No,' replies Nafisa. 'This column is for date, then time, then name of station calling, then name of caller and name of person replying. Then message. That is how we did it when I worked for W.H.O.' Nafisa takes over the writing of the column headings.

I place the book beside the radio, open at the first page. 'OK, starting with the next call we write it down, yes?'

'I know that,' replies Nafisa, 'it's Zia who needs to remember.' She casts a look of rebuke in his direction.

Zia grins and looks at his feet. 'I will do it,' he mutters.

A short while later, Zia brings in a visitor. 'Hafizi is here to see you.'

Hafizi is dressed in a grey-green *shalwar* suit with a brown waistcoat. His hair and moustache are completely white. His face is tense, even when he smiles.

'My name is Hafizi, I'm the manager of the Phul-i-Khumri office.'

We sit in the central square of the bungalow and Zia comes to join us.

In the diffused sunlight that penetrates the dome over our heads, Musa serves glasses of tea and a small, silver tray of sweets.

Hafizi takes out his handkerchief and wipes the sweat from his forehead. 'You see, Eileen, the fighting in Phul-i-Khumri was so fierce, I could not bear to think of my two lovely daughters and my wife and mother-in-law in such danger and we moved to Kabul. I have brought the accounts books with me so you can inspect them.'

'Thank you, Hafizi, just leave them on the table. I'll take a look later. How do you feel about your move to Kabul?'

'My mother-in-law is very old. When we left I had to carry her to the car on my back. I'm afraid this move away from home will kill her. I am very worried for my children. My five-year-old daughter clings to her mother all the time and whenever there is a sudden sound, she buries her head in her mother's clothes and cries. We are letting her sleep with us in our bed. She wakes up screaming two or three times every night. My wife is exhausted.'

'What would you like to do now?' I ask.

'I am renting rooms in Kabul but now Kabul is worse than Phul-i-Khumri. I will probably take my family back there soon.'

After tea and conversation, Hafizi mops his forehead with his handkerchief again. 'Excuse me, Eileen, I need to return to my family.'

'Of course, Hafizi, please give my *salaams*, regards, to your wife.'

I return to my list of tasks. 'We need to start using this mileage book.' I open the standard issue Oxfam mileage book to show them.

Nafisa's eyes brighten with recognition. 'We kept a book like this one when I worked for W.H.O. Every Thursday it was my job to check it. I had to find where someone had driven for his private use and bill him for the miles. We should do the same here, too.'

'Yes, Nafisa, you are right.'

Nafisa looks sternly at Zia like a mother admonishing her child. 'Zia, you must remember this. Ehsan also drives. He must do it, too.'

In rapid Dari, Nafisa gives Ehsan sharp instructions on how to use the book. Ehsan nods from time to time, apparently expressing his understanding.

Nafisa finds a ballpoint pen and a piece of string which she attaches to the pen and the book. 'No-one must take the pen!' she commands as she takes the book to put into the Suzuki.

So far so good. I cross another item off my list. I think I can see what is happening here. Nafisa knows how things should be done, she just needs some help to stand her ground in keeping the men on track.

'The problem is, Eileen,' says Nafisa, 'Zia and Ehsan are not the real drivers. The driver disappeared a month ago. He was kidnapped by a militia. We don't know which group or where he is. Zia made many enquiries. It was no use, we could not find him. So now Zia and Ehsan drive.'

What do I say in reply to this new reminder of the perils that lie outside these four walls? Nothing comes to me except an increased admiration for the Afghan staff who come to work despite the dangers.

The guard, Babur, comes to the door.

'He is saying Mr Rasheed is here to see you,' says Zia.

Zia, Mr Rasheed and I go to the reception area under the dome.

'I live in the house next door. I've come to welcome you to Kabul.'

'Thank you, Mr Rasheed. I'm very pleased to meet you.'

Musa brings more glasses of tea and another silver saucer of sweets.

'I am the owner of this property, your landlord. I have a portfolio of property in Kabul that I let out for offices and homes.'

'It must be difficult managing property in these conditions.'

'Exactly. It was a good living until all this destruction started. Now, I don't know from one day to the next whether my properties are still standing.'

Mr Rasheed is small, for a man. His face is smiling and kindly. He's wearing a white *shalwar* suit and an embroidered cap.

'Here is my business card. If you need anything, you must tell me. Michael visited about a month ago. I understand he is bringing some people for a visit to Kabul?'

'Yes, he mentioned it to me, too, when I was in Islamabad. He asked me to make the arrangements.'

'Exactly. He asked me to provide ten sleeping mats, quilts, pillows, plates and all these things. I will bring them if you wish but surely he won't bring people into these conditions? It would be madness.'

Zia and I look at each other.

'I'm not sure,' I reply, 'I'll be writing to him in the next day or two. I'll advise him of the conditions and ask for his response.'

'Well, please do tell me as soon as possible, I need to know. I don't want to buy ten sleeping mats if they are not going to be used.'

Zia and Mr Rasheed chat for a while about common acquaintances, those who are staying, leaving, injured, or have died. Then Mr Rasheed leaves to go about his business.

'There is difficulty,' says Zia. 'Guard, Samimi, is holding political meeting in guards' room. There are five people in there with him but his party is not party that holds this street. Is very dangerous.'

'And he is threatening the women staff too much,' adds Nafisa. 'He says Mr Michael told him to make this house his home. Samimi says he doesn't allow women to be unveiled in his house and will not allow us to be unveiled here. He says he will rape the women who are unveiled. That's me and you, Eileen.'

'When guards, Samimi and Babur, were taken on,' says Zia, 'they were armed. Problem was they are from different group than group that controls street. It was... *er*...'

'Provocative,' Nafisa suggests.

'Yes. Even guards themselves said it was dangerous. We had to take guns apart and hide them in loft.'

'You should dismiss him, Eileen,' says Nafisa.

'No,' Zia retorts. 'He receives the good fee. There is no other work for him. He will not wish to go. He has influence over his Mujahedeen group and they can carry out his threats. It is the dangerous situation. To fire him will make it worse.'

Musa speaks. Zia translates, 'Musa says he will protect you with his life. At night he will place his sleeping mat outside your door and if anyone tries to step over him they will have to kill him first.'

'Please tell Musa I am grateful for his offer of protection but I hope there will be no need for anyone to be killed.'

We hear voices coming to the door. Zia goes to greet the visitors. It's a group of men who were refugees in Pakistan. Now they have returned. Zia brings them to the central square, introduces me and we all sit down on the sofa and chairs.

'They are afraid their money will be stolen if they carry it back from Peshawar. They deposit money with Mr Michael in Islamabad and we repay them when they come here,' Zia says.

'How do you know how much to give them?' I ask.

'Mr Michael sends me the *sitor* with amount and when they will arrive I prepare money for them.'

'*Sitor*?'

'Yes, Mrs Eileen, it is the written message through computer connected to radio.'

Zia chats to the men, asking them about their journey. The leader of the group hands Zia a piece of paper and Zia goes to the safe.

Under the watchful eyes of the group, Zia counts out the money, note by note, onto the table. The leader picks up the bundle and counts it again. There is a unanimous grunt of approval and the leader puts the cash into a pocket inside his tunic.

With handshakes for Zia, nods to me and right-fist-on-heart salutes, they take their leave.

'Nafisa, please look at the new cash book I've set up.'

'Yes. It is the same as before.'

'Mostly. Look at this last column.'

'*Balance in hand*. That is the cash we have in the safe?'

'Yes. Each time you make an entry in the book, you also write in the amount that is left. At any time, we can count the money and check that it agrees with the book.'

'Yes, I can do that. What does it mean, *voucher number*?'

'For every entry in the cash book, there must be something to show what came in or went out - a receipt, a bill, an invoice. That's called a *voucher*. You put a number here, starting with number one. Write the same number on the voucher then file it in number order.'

'So we can check that the money went correctly.'

'Yes.'

'One more thing, Nafisa. There has been a problem in the past that too many people have been writing in the cash book. From now on, I want only you to write in the cash book for the Afghani currency. You'll remember what you've done, so there is less risk of something going in twice or being left out.'

'Oh, yes, Eileen. It will make me too much happy to do this.'

'You need to count the cash at least at the end of each week and make sure the actual cash in the safe agrees the running balance in the book. If it doesn't agree, if it's *out*, you have to check it all over to find the mistake and put it right. If you get stuck, you can ask me to help. Remember, no one else may write anything in the book, except for me when I check it. I'll sign and date it, then we'll both know it's correct at that point.

'I will do that, starting today. I won't get stuck. You'll see I can do it. You will come and inspect it, a surprise check when I don't know you are coming, that is how we did it at W.H.O. and then you will know I am doing everything exactly as you say.'

'Yes, Nafisa. I'll do that. I'll also check that the cash book is linked to the vouchers' file through the numbers.'

For the time being, I'm only giving Nafisa responsibility for Afghani currency. I'll keep control of the dollars' account myself until I see how she gets on. I intend to make a spot check of the book, vouchers and cash many times over the next few months. Nafisa is so intelligent and keen to learn, I'm expecting to find everything in perfect order.

The lull in the fighting today has been a welcome relief. It's been a good day.

Thursday 23rd July 1992, Kabul, Afghanistan

To: Michael Semple
From: Eileen Masters
WEEKLY REPORT No.1.

Greetings from Kabul! Although it is not yet a week, I am advised that we must send our post today to catch this week's flight.

The journey took a total of 15.5 hours. I will not go into all the details but we were held up at the border for some time. Zia found it difficult to drive the Suzuki in places.

Although it was quiet when we arrived at 8.15 pm on Saturday, large areas of the city were caught in rocket cross-fire which began at 2 am on Sunday and continued until 9 pm on Monday. It was quieter on Tuesday but Wednesday was the first day since my arrival on which we were able to work normally.

With help from Zia I have started to use the radio and have set up a radio log to log all calls both incoming and outgoing. I am in the process of setting up stock control records and personnel records, which should be fully in operation starting next week. The vehicle mileage log is now in use. Nafisa is working on the list of emergency contact details requested by Oxford.

It has not been possible to achieve a great deal this week due to the conditions. The bank opened for the first time on Wednesday.

Due to the rocket attacks, staff attendance has been low. I was concerned that Zia and Nafisa have been taking considerable personal risks by travelling in.

All the staff have difficult family situations. Some have had to evacuate their homes and others have had to receive friends and relatives from the battle zone. I have spent some time counselling staff who have been in a state of anxiety.

Nafisa has a good understanding of the principles of running an office though she needs some guidance in methods. Although it is early yet, I am hopeful that over the next few months I can coach her to run the office effectively.

Hafizi has been here since before I arrived on Saturday. Hafizi has also had to evacuate his family from their home and plans to stay in Kabul until the situation settles.

I intend to give Hafizi a fixed float of one million Afghanis (approximately £1,000). His expenditure will be reimbursed on production of his accounts to restore his float to its original level.

While it is quiet at present, I suggest reconsideration of your plans to hold the workshop here. If you decide nevertheless to come, please let us have full details and numbers asap.

We did not discuss what you wanted by way of reports from me or what reports you have been used to receiving from here. It would help me to have some feedback from you on this report. Please indicate whether you require more or less information than is given in this report and whether you wish the reports to continue weekly or monthly.

Regards to all,
Eileen

Thursday 23rd July 1992, Kabul, Afghanistan

I have always enjoyed learning myself and it gives me great pleasure to help others learn. I love seeing their delight when they discover they can do something new. It's especially rewarding with Zia, Nafisa and Ehsan being so keen and quick to learn. As I tick off the items on their training list that we've covered so far, I remember an impromptu lesson I gave in Sukkur, Pakistan, six years ago.

1986, Sukkur, Sindh, Pakistan

'Good morning, Madam.'

'Good morning, girls. Please sit down.'

That was the easy bit. Class 10B girls looked at me and I looked at the expectant faces of class 10B girls. The only warning I'd been given that I was to teach the class was no more than minutes previously when the usual maths teacher was taken ill. In my usual *have a go* style, I accepted the unexpected commission. I had no idea what I was going to teach them.

A girl from class 10B was summoned to the headmaster's office and instructed to take me to the classroom. As we walked along the verandah, I asked her where they had got to in their books and hoped it was a subject I could remember. I looked at the book. *Ah*. Algebra. Yes, I had a vague memory of it.

The scent of sweating bodies wafted out through the open windows and door. Although most classes had 75 to 100 students in them, this was the matriculation grade and entry to it was by examination so there were only 36 in this class. The girls sat with their white veils covering their heads, three to a desk designed for two, despite the heat. A single ceiling fan tried, rather ineffectively, to stir up the hot air as I looked at the one antiquated text book:

> *'The process of multiplication of two terms depends upon the commutative and associative properties of multiplication and distributive property of multiplication over addition. If two terms are multiplied then the exponents of the variables are added up and their coefficients are multiplied together.'*

72

I decided to abandon the text book and do it my way. I picked up the chalk and approached the blackboard sideways on so that most of the class could see what I was writing. I wrote:

$2^2 \times 2^3$

$a^2 \times a^3$

We worked through these two examples, expanding the expressions into a series of five multiplied numbers, drew from them the basic principle and went on to the more complex exercises in the book.

The class was a pleasure to teach. Whenever I asked a question, the girls stretched their hands high above their heads, eager to give the answers.

I don't know whether the girls of class 10B learned anything from the lesson that day but I loved their enthusiasm and energy for study.

Thursday 23rd July 1992, Kabul, Afghanistan

There are voices outside and another visitor is ushered in.

'Hi, I'm Jolyon Leslie, Habitat. Welcome to Kabul!'

'Hi, Eileen Masters, great to meet you.'

I observe a man who appears slightly younger than me. He has blond hair, blue eyes, a confident manner and a South African accent.

'I've brought a copy of a report I wrote, a project evaluation. I've sent one to Michael. I heard you were here and I thought you might like to see it.' He hands me a black plastic folder.

'Yes, I'd like to read it, get my head into gear with what's what.'

'I hear you're living over the shop. Done that myself a few times. Not easy.'

'More like, *in* the shop, in my case. It has its advantages, though. I can potter around doing bits of work in the evenings and weekends.'

'You should move over to the UNOCA Staff House. You'd be safer there. I'd give you a room in my house but I've just moved my office in. Easier in these conditions.'

'UNOCA Staff House?'

'Yes, Zia'll know where it is. There's a guesthouse, swimming pool, squash court, small restaurant. Most internationals go there, especially on Fridays.'

Jolyon tells me he's been in Afghanistan for three years, apart from a few months when he broke his leg and had to go to Pakistan for treatment.

I offer coffee.

Jolyon says he can't stay. 'A lot to catch up on while it's quiet. You learn to do what you can, while you can, out here. What's possible today might not be possible tomorrow.'

Jolyon walks to the door shaking his head. 'Sheer insanity, being next to the Ministry of the Interior. You should find somewhere safer.'

CHAPTER 8: IN THE CROSSFIRE

Monday 27th July 1992, Kabul, Afghanistan

Today there is a lull. Only the occasional, distant *boom* reminds me that this is a city at war with itself.

Zia declares it safe to make a trip to the bank. We need to obtain Afghan currency and the withdrawal needs my signature. Zia and I climb into the cab of the little Suzuki pick-up and he drives us the short distance to the Da Afghanistan Bank.

At one time, Kabul was a thriving city and a popular tourist spot, a place of convergence for overlanders travelling from Europe to Asia. Now most of its attractions are destroyed by years of war. Large numbers of its inhabitants have fled. Those who are left struggle to survive in what remains of the city.

Today, people have emerged from their sheltering places and life appears almost normal. Roadside stalls are open, each claiming the shade of one of the mulberry trees that line the streets. Sellers have set out their wares on the pavement – a display of sweets spread on a cloth on the ground, a table of dusty apples, a mound of second-hand clothes. Behind them shops are open, everything from shed-like stalls to glamorous department stores.

'You know, Mrs Eileen,' says Zia, 'every day we make decision. We will hide from rockets, or we will earn our salaries. Today is earn our salaries.'

Zia must do the business transaction. It must be a man, of course, and I accept it as a gesture of respect to me when, in the unlit bank, they lead me to wait at the desk of a lady clerk. The sign over her head says *Foreign Payments*. She signals with her chin to a man in a grey *shalwar* suit. He brings a wooden chair, ceremoniously flicks a grubby duster over it and places it beside her. I sit down.

'Good morning, Madam, I am Razia.'

'Good morning, Razia, I am Eileen.'

Razia's black eyebrows hop up and down in a nervous tick. She signals again with her chin to the man in the grey *shalwar* suit and shortly afterwards he comes with two glasses of orange-coloured tea. Her eyebrows are still for a moment as she takes a sip of tea.

'Both houses next of mine are badly damaged. By the grace of Almighty Allah we are saved. Now, food is difficult. Is no wheat-flour! How I can feed my family when I can't make naan bread? Usually my husband's brother helps us. He was the high-up at the Interior Ministry, you know, but when fighters took over the building, he had to leave. He took his family out to Peshawar. Now we have no-one to help us, no-one.' She wipes a tear from her eye with the corner of her scarf.

'You know, Madam, I come to work every day but we do not receive salary now, not for three months.'

Zia finishes the business transaction and comes for me. Back in the Suzuki, I stifle a giggle as I contemplate what he will say if we are stopped with the stash of money in the back. What would he make me this time? A simpleton wife, a doctor, or something even more imaginative?

Monday 27th July 1992, Oxford, U.K.

Dear Eileen,

I heard there were some fireworks shortly after you arrived! I wonder what your accommodation is like.

Miracle of miracles, my last pay packet contained my tax refund and not a moment too soon. Unfortunately, they'd only paid me for 30 hours, not the 50 I was due. I called in at the factory office and thanked the lady who does the wages for the tax refund and queried the underpayment. She said she was sorry and hoped I would understand. I said I did but would appreciate a cheque for the difference if she wouldn't mind. So while I waited, she went and found the boss (her dad) for his signature on the cheque.

Saturday I was at a barbeque held at the boss's house. (The barbeque had originally been intended as his daughter's wedding reception until she called the wedding off!) We all stood around the swimming pool pretending to be relaxed, equal and chummy. There was plenty of nice food and drink.

I have had to book two of my weeks' holiday as they have to be taken before November. The other week we have to take at Christmas when the factory closes down. I've booked 10th to 24th August. I hope to be visiting family on some weekends while Saturdays are free. I can also get the guttering done now the bank account is a bit healthier.

Today I have been at Great Milton playing for ballet exams – actually it was modern and tap this time.

Jon, Dan and Mandy are all here and are well apart from Mandy's back problem. Her doctor is arranging to get her checked up at the hospital. No date yet.

Puss Puss has started contributing food for the household now – she left a headless mouse on the doorstep yesterday. I think she was a bit put out that we didn't eat it straight away after the trouble she'd gone to!

To date I've received your two faxes and one letter.

Are you getting enough tea?

Goodbye for now.

Be good.

Love

Alan

Thursday 30th July 1992, Kabul, Afghanistan

The Afghan staff sit in strict pecking order down each side of the table while I sit at the head. I find the arrangement uncomfortable. This, however, is the way things are done and I've been in the region long enough to know better than to try to impose my own culture on others. The dining room is vibrating to the sound of explosions outside. Musa brings trays of stew and rice. A few minutes of silence follow as everyone tucks into their lunch.

Next to me on the men's side of the table is Zia. Next to Zia sits Ehsan. Ehsan has the pale complexion and oriental face of a Hazara, a distinct ethnic group that traces its roots back to Alexander the Great. Ehsan speaks calmly, almost too quietly to hear, as Zia interprets.

'He is saying his brother's family has moved in with him because shelling destroyed brother's house. Overcrowding is difficult for his wife, who has to cook for them all. He says he used to allow his wife to be unveiled in home. Now she has to wear shawl over her head always because she is in presence of her husband's men relatives.'

Nafisa scowls at this information.

I ask whether Musa will join us. Nafisa tells me he takes his lunch with Samimi and Babur in the guards' room by the gate.

On the women's side of the table is Nafisa. I'm to train her in Oxfam methods of accounting, make her an expert at keeping the books and running the office. Gulshad, the lady who does the cleaning and helps Musa in the kitchen, sits next to Nafisa.

Nafisa interprets as Gulshad says she is worried about her children.

'I used to have a nice home. My husband had a good job in an office and earned good salaries. One day, a rocket hit our house. He was killed, stone cold dead, right there where he was sitting. One side of our house was completely destroyed. Without my husband, I didn't know how I will get food for my children. I thought I would have to go to my husband's brother. Many places will not employ women. By the grace of

Almighty Allah, Mr Michael gave me this job. I am too much grateful. Now I can live with my eight children in the room that is still standing.'

Gulshad says that she locks the children in the house while she comes to work. Last night, the shock wave of a rocket exploding nearby smashed her window. Her children were playing outside and she was crazy with panic until she had gathered them indoors. Today, she has to leave her children with a neighbour. She's not happy about it. She doesn't trust her neighbour to keep them safe. She shows us her hands, red and grazed from clearing up the broken glass.

Gulshad is very thin. I wonder whether she has enough to eat. I long to move her up to my end of the table, to have her sit next to me, to show her that I value her, but I know that if I interfere, the other staff will feel devalued and demoted and Gulshad would be too embarrassed to change her place in this strictly stratified society.

Outside, the thuds and thumps intensify while we make conversation. I tell them about a scene in the film *Carry on up the Khyber* in which the characters are having lunch while a battle rages around them. The staff smile politely. They are not really amused. They have survived years of war. They've eaten innumerable meals to the sounds of battle.

A large amount of food has been prepared, more than sufficient for all of us. I know that after the meal some plausible-sounding reason will divert my attention. The staff will invisibly slip food into plastic containers to take home to their families. Under Oxfam rules, this is not allowed. The meal is part of the local job package to ensure that staff have at least one meal each day, along with medical expenses and 'pick up, drop off' transport so the women can get to work safely, but Kabul is under siege. Food is rotting on lorries waiting to enter the city. Inside Kabul, food is scarce, prices are soaring and their children are hungry. So I'll pretend I haven't heard the whispers or the plastic lids snapping closed or the furtive trips to where the coats and *burqas* are hanging.

The staff know their thumps and thuds. While the lunchtime noises are loud, they declare them to be 'outgoing' and seem unconcerned. Now the timbre changes and their faces become tense as they turn to look out of the windows and declare the new *booms* to be 'incoming'.

Nafisa raises the ever-present walkie-talkie to her ear. 'The U.N. are going to their bunkers.'

I ask Zia, 'Do you think we should go to the shelter?'

'If you wish.'

'What do you think, Nafisa?'

'U.N. are all in their bunkers now.'

'OK,' I say, 'let's go down.'

The bunker, our shelter from the air raids, is in the garden. It looks like a brick anorak hood standing up over the grass with steps going down into a brick-lined hole. There's no door and no sandbags to absorb the shockwave of a blast. Zia and Ehsan insist on bringing down some chairs. They come and go until six chairs are placed in a circle in the underground igloo.

A thunderous *boom* rocks our simple shelter, shaking the ground like an earth tremor.

Nafisa still has the walkie-talkie close to her ear. 'That was near the Staff House, a kilometre from here.'

Gulshad wants to go home to her children. It's understandable, any mother would. I try to persuade her to stay a little longer. It wouldn't be safe to go out now.

Musa comes down the steps carrying a large kettle of tea and a tray of glasses. To the background rumbles and crashes, we drink tea.

Nafisa says, 'We should keep candles down here in case we need to come down when it's dark.'

'Ehsan says we must not forget matches to light candles,' adds Zia.

I ask Zia if we can get a door fitted to the bunker or make a blast wall of sandbags to protect the entrance. Zia and Ehsan have a short discussion in Dari and Zia tells me Ehsan has a cousin who can supply us with sand and another who can bring some sacks. I ask them to arrange it as soon as possible.

The thumps and thuds are less frequent now. Nafisa says the U.N. are still in their bunkers. Gulshad is anxious to get back to her children. Zia says he will drive her home in the Suzuki and we all go back into the office.

I feel safer indoors. The rooms are more enclosed than the bunker with its open entrance, though I like to be well away from the glass dome. It's almost time for the staff to go home anyway, and Zia will drive them all.

Thinking I'm alone, except for the guards at the gate, I sit at my desk and start checking the cash book.

Musa appears at the door, 'Tea, Madam?'

'Yes, please, Musa. Tea would be lovely.'

Friday 31st July 1992, Kabul, Afghanistan

'My tea is nearly ready and the sun has left the sky...' I say aloud the poem learned when I was ten years old. Friday is the Afghan day off. I'm alone in the bunker. I have to keep my mind occupied, block out what's going on around me.

'Doe ik'm doe' I recite the two times table in Punjabi, learned in Sukkur to help the hostel boys with their homework.

My isolation is pressing in on me more heavily with each explosion. I have to concentrate on something else, to keep my mind occupied, to keep sanity on the inside and insanity on the outside. I name the five rivers of the Punjab, count down from one thousand in sevens.

I never really know who is fighting whom at any given time. It seems to me that they fire their weapons at random and whatever they hit, they call the target.

'Khudaavan mera chopaan hai,' The twenty-third Psalm I learned in an Urdu lesson in Sukkur, Pakistan.

Don't think, don't think, blot it out. 'I have a little shadow that goes in and out with me...'

Saturday 1st August 1992, Kabul, Afghanistan

The staff come to the office today despite the noise outside.

'That's not for us,' says Zia, 'they are attacking airport. Is some miles from here. *Hisbe Islami* militia has put out on radio that it is their reply to government's attacks yesterday.'

'I'm confused. Yesterday's was a government attack?'

'Yes, Mrs Eileen.'

'The government is blitzing its own people? I don't understand any of this.'

Today, I write the second report to Michael and again ask him to reconsider his plans to bring the Pakistani staff for a workshop. Zia is risking his life going out to send my reports and *sitors* through the U.N. offices. Each time he goes, Zia checks for Michael's replies. He only finds messages reiterating that Michael is coming and the workshop will take place.

'Problem is, Islamabad staff are not used to these conditions,' says Zia. 'Last time there was the war in Pakistan was 1973. Most, they are too young to remember it. How they will manage here?'

'Well, Zia, the way I see it, we've sent him two *sitors* telling him what's happening and asking him to reconsider. I've also spelled it out in my reports. Maybe he doesn't read them, maybe he's ignoring them, or perhaps he just doesn't believe it's as bad as I say. We must let him come and see for himself.'

'Let him come into this, with all those young people?'

I remember the question that Pat from Personnel asked at my interview. 'What would you do if your manager told you to do something that you thought was unreasonable? If he wouldn't listen, if he couldn't understand your side of things at all?'

'We can't stop him,' I reply, 'At the end of the day, he's the boss and he can do what he likes.'

Zia is such a private person. He's never mentioned his family. I respect his wish for privacy and don't pry. He's not one for showing his feelings, either. The complete opposite to Nafisa, only his eyes speak of his anxiety, his empathy with and concern for others, his understanding of how things work and how to get something done. Right now I see discontent in his eyes. He's not happy with my answer.

Sunday 2nd August 1992, Oxford, U.K.

Dear Eileen,

How are you doing? The weather has continued dry here and quite warm at times.

Jon had Bryony over for a few days. He's run out of money again so he worked at County Dairies today and will again tomorrow.

Dan has now bought a new drum machine that can play by itself! He baked and iced a sponge cake yesterday. He succeeded with a technique that involves sticking pins all around halfway up the side of the cake and laying numerous strands of icing out to the ends of the pins. It all stayed in place when he took the pins out. I wish he wouldn't keep licking the nozzles while he's using them.

There's no news of Mandy's hospital appointment yet. She seems to be managing on the painkillers the doctor prescribed.

I took Dan and Mandy to Finmere Market today. I wanted to get a new hose for the vacuum cleaner but there was no stall selling that kind of thing. Dan bought a leather-look jacket.

Puss Puss seems to prefer staying out most nights. She knows she can always climb in Jon's window if it rains.

I cut that useless shrub down to the ground – the one that produces two mangy apologies for flowers per year.

It has been an expensive week what with the telephone bill and the road fund licence, which I renewed for a year. However, Dan and and Mandy's rent just about covered them.

There haven't been any TV or radio reports from where you are. Does that mean it is quiet?

Take care

Love

Alan

CHAPTER 9: NO TIME TO GO ANYWHERE

Wednesday 5th August 1992, Kabul, Afghanistan

'Yes, Sir, I will pass on message. Over and out.'

Zia puts down the microphone, makes a note in the log book and turns away from the radio.

'Mrs Eileen, you remember I went to U.N. offices to report your arrival?'

'Yes, Zia, I remember.'

'They are asking you will return this afternoon while Kabul is quiet. They want to speak you.'

The security officer spoke bluntly. 'The United Nations only offers protection or assistance to those who have an existing contractual agreement and there is no such agreement with Oxfam. This is no place for a woman. Get out while you still can. And get Oxfam's communications sorted. We didn't mind helping out when Oxfam was first setting up but it's been going on for three years now and you're still dependent on us to pass messages between you and your Islamabad office. It's time Oxfam got its own communications equipment and stood on its own two feet.'

As things turn out, there's no time to go anywhere.

Thursday 6th August 1992, Kabul, Afghanistan

There are some rather disturbing aspects of a rocket attack. It tends to build up slowly from an occasional, thunderous roll to something fierce. It is just as well that there is a warning time while it intensifies, as the decision of whether or not to go to the bunker is a difficult one. If we go down too soon it means a lot of hanging about down there when there isn't much activity. The walkie-talkie is a big help. When the U.N. issues a message to all stations telling everyone to go to their cellars we know it's time to move.

It seems we have just reached a critical point as Musa has ushered me down to the bunker. Of course, now we have descended it has gone much quieter. *Whoops.* Perhaps not. One of the guards, Babur, has now come down. It's not too bad today and I'm glad to have Musa and Babur with me. I don't know where the other guard, Samimi, is. He apparently prefers to trust his fate above ground. Perhaps Allah has predestined him to be *shaheed*, a martyr.

A good coating of insect repellent is essential, as the bunker is where the mosquitoes go for a meal out. I have assigned specific tasks to everyone. Nafisa and Gulshad will bring candles and matches, Zia and Ehsan will bring chairs. None of them is here today. They couldn't leave their homes because of the blitz.

Musa is coming down the steps with a kettle of tea and glasses on a tray. This time I have brought my diary with me. If I write about it, it will be on the outside, something I am describing from a distance.

The trouble with the rockets is the silence. First there's a thud as they are fired, followed by a whirring sound. That part is OK because you can judge where they are. Then comes the silence. At this point you have no idea how close they are and have to make a decision whether to stay upright or hit the floor. Then you hear the explosion. Next come the wails – slow, high-pitched songs of agony and lament. A siren is sounding, I think it's an ambulance.

The attack gradually dies away in the same waves as it came and we emerge into the dusty garden.

Thursday 6th August 1992, Kabul, Afghanistan

To: Michael Semple

From: Eileen Masters

WEEKLY REPORT No.3

The week has been dominated by the security situation. There has been regular fighting in the evenings with heavy artillery and rockets. The U.N. planned an evacuation but had to suspend it as the airport had to be closed.

I wish to record here that I have twice included in *sitors* to you a message to reconsider your plans to come but that you have nevertheless indicated your intention to come. I then asked you by *sitor* to radio before you leave Islamabad. To date I have not heard from you.

Very little has been achieved this week. The new cash book and vouchers are now operational.

Gulshad has been absent for two days as her house was damaged by one of this week's rocket attacks. I am not sure whether Samimi has left us temporarily or permanently. At present except for one guard, Babur, I am entirely alone here as there are no staff in at all today.

Friday 7th August 1992, Kabul, Afghanistan

Today, Kabul is quiet and I'm tired of being alone. The only social gathering place I know is the UNOCA Staff House (United Nations Office for the Co-ordination of Assistance Programmes in Afghanistan).

Zia isn't around. As in most Islamic countries, Friday is the national day off and Zia deserves his rest day. I climb into Suzie, the Suzuki, and try to remember how to drive. Although I passed my driving test at the second attempt in 1980, I haven't actually driven a car in the twelve years since.

'Come on, Suzie, don't let me down,' I say aloud as I place a foot on the clutch and turn the ignition. The engine fires up.

Ah. Zia must have forgotten to remove the spark plugs. Good start because I don't know how to put them back in.

I peer at the gear stick. It looks like first gear is up and to the left. I give it a push. It stays where it is. I push again, harder. Suzie jolts as it clunks into place. Suzie and I grind our way out of the compound and onto the road. Now I have to change to second. Foot off gas and onto clutch. Push, harder this time, into second. Suzie flinches. Foot back onto gas. Suzie doesn't like this and hops, skips and jumps all the way to the Staff House.

The U.N. boys drink lager and swim in the pool. I prefer a cup of tea, lounging at the poolside, and chatting with a lady from the International Committee of the Red Cross, while listening to the relaxing sound of splashing water.

Then the familiar booming comes from the hills. Voices say, 'Incoming. Better go now.' The pool empties, belongings are packed into bags. A line of vehicles leaves the compound and Suzie hops, skips and jumps along the road to home.

Saturday 8th August, Kabul, Afghanistan

'Once fifteen is fifteen, two fifteens are thirty.' Artillery shells are crashing down on Kabul. I'm in the bunker in the garden. I have only my faithful numbers to blot out the mayhem around me.

'Three fifteens are forty-five.' At least I'm not entirely alone. Opposite me, Babur, the only member of staff here today, sits on his haunches, reading a book.

'Four fifteens are sixty,'

An almighty blast rocks the ground, the shockwave crashes into my body, something inside my ears gives way.

'*Naz-deek aast.*' That's close, says Babur.

I hear voices on the walkie-talkie. I raise it to my ear.

I hear a South African accented voice, I recognise it as Jolyon Leslie. His normally calm demeanour is betrayed by his shouts of high-pitched distress, 'They're hit, they're hit, we need a doctor, at once!'

Then I hear the controlled voice of the British U.N. security officer, 'What is your location?'

'Outside my house. My Afghan staff, they were leaving in the vehicle to go home and it took a hit.'

'Get back in your bunker. Stay inside.'

'I'm staying with them. Two dead, two seriously wounded. We need urgent medical assistance.'

The voice of New Zealand U.N. officer, John Tacon, joins the conversation. 'I'm on my way over. I'll bring my boy-scout first aid box. If I can find it.'

'This is suicidal, get back in your bunkers!'

I listen as Jolyon and John go out under the fiery sky. John picks up the wounded and takes them to the hospital for whatever help he may be able to find. Jolyon takes the bodies of the dead back home to their families, staying a while to grieve with them.

This could happen to Oxfam staff. We have no medical back-up. Kabul hospitals have no drugs or equipment. Even the Red Cross drug store and sterilisation unit have taken a direct hit and hospitals are under the control of the Mujahedeen who only allow their own supporters to be treated.

Ignoring Babur's gestures to stay in the bunker, I come up into the office. I need to think. I do that best with a cup of tea. I go into the kitchen. There's no electricity. I find a match, light the gas and put the kettle on. Telephones are cut off. A blockade of the city means no food, and no banks or shops are open. It's impossible to work but the Oxfam programme is desperately needed and, right now, it's my responsibility to keep it going. I wrap the handle of the boiling kettle in a tea-towel and pour the hot water onto the tea leaves in the mug. The bombardment increases in tempo.

Babur, the guard who was with me in the bunker, comes in.

'Samimi,' he says. He flicks his hand backwards to gesture *gone*. Then he points to himself and makes the gesture again. I understand. He wants to leave and Samimi has already deserted his post.

I pick up a pen and write on a scrap of paper: *I am a woman alone here. Please may I come to your house?*

I look at Babur. I point toward the paper and then toward the house next door. 'Mr Rasheed,' I say. 'Then you go.' On the last three words I point to Babur and make the *gone* gesture that he used.

Babur nods. I hand him the paper. He gives a right-fist-on-heart salute.

'*Khuda hafiz.*' God protect you, I say.

Does he understand me? Will he deliver the note to Mr Rasheed, or will he be in such a hurry to get to his family that he won't do it?

I'll give him fifteen minutes then I'll just get my handbag, walk next door and trust myself to Afghan hospitality.

Only moments after I have dispatched Babur with my note, Mr Rasheed arrives. As he walks me to his house, he tells me that he's already sent his wife and children to Peshawar. His sisters are still here. They will look after me.

Mr Rasheed's sisters are sitting on a red carpet on the hallway floor, well away from any windows. He apologises for not being able to treat me as he likes to treat guests but this is the safest place. I check in on the walkie-talkie to report my new whereabouts and ask for the information to be relayed to Michael in Islamabad.

Sunday 9th August 1992, Kabul, Afghanistan

The sky is ablaze, artillery resounds from the hills and the ground trembles as rockets boom, swish and crash. Mr Rasheed's sisters sit quietly, occasionally venturing into the kitchen and returning with glasses of sweet-spiced tea or red cherry juice. The call to prayer sounds over the din. The Rasheeds align their mats to face the east and pray for Allah's mercy.

The sisters set out a white tablecloth on the floor and place on it dishes of hot chicken and vegetable stew with rice. They give a white dinner plate to Mr Rasheed and one to me.

'Please, eat,' says Mr Rasheed.

'Are your sisters going to join us?' I ask.

Mr Rasheed laughs and translates my question for his sisters. Then he interprets their reply into English.

'They are saying they have too much respect for their brother to eat with him.'

They're treating me as an honorary man, as often happens in Afghan and Pakistani homes. I always feel uncomfortable when I have to eat first while the women wait but this is their custom and I am in their home.

I ask for a spoon. I don't want to spoil Mr Rasheed's nice carpet. I put some rice and stew on my plate, being careful to leave plenty in the serving dishes for the sisters.

When Mr Rasheed and I have finished, the sisters enjoy their meal. They don't need such fripperies as plates and spoons. They adeptly eat the rice and stew from the serving dishes with their fingers without dropping a single grain of rice.

Mr Rasheed listens to the BBC Pashto service, relaying the news to me in English. Now he's staring at the radio in his hand as if he can't believe what he's hearing.

'Today's attacks are from Hekmatyar's forces... They are saying a thousand, more than a thousand rockets have hit Kabul city... The airport has more than 250 hits... A thousand people are killed...'

The worst part is the feeling of helplessness. I don't mind danger if I'm achieving something. Here, no one can do anything. What's the point of it all? Why am I here if I can do nothing other than sit in hiding amid the destruction of a foreign city?

Sunday 9th August 1992, Oxford, U.K.

Dear Eileen,

It's the first day of my holiday today and I've made a start on the guttering. It is all assembled and temporarily in place but I shall take down and give the fascia board a new coat of white paint before the final fixing.

Jon has got work for three days at the nearby Oxford Business Park sorting out computer disks and labelling them.

We are all being bitten by fleas lately. No, not because the cleaning is being neglected but because a period of warm, humid weather has caused widespread infestations of the little beggars. The pet shops are doing a roaring trade in household flea sprays. I'm going to blitz the whole house tomorrow while everyone is out. I tried hoovering the whole house in one go last weekend but they're still biting. Even Puss Puss races across the floor and jumps up onto the nearest high-up refuge.

The factory is taking on new work for Nissan and Honda cars. The boss told us all last week that business is growing and that we'll be recruiting new staff soon. He recognised that we were all working to full capacity.

Dan and Mandy are busy getting ready for their fortnight's caravan holiday. Mandy was in bed all day yesterday with her bad back – she's still waiting for a hospital appointment.

As I was writing this, the 1 pm news reported the latest Kabul news. I immediately phoned Islamabad. Michael said you are OK and he is putting arrangements in place for you to leave if necessary.

My mother phoned today. She has heard the Kabul news items on the BBC. I told her what I knew. The main news is mostly of Sarajevo civil war and Somalia famine. Kabul comes right at the very end if there is time left. Or else I listen to the World Service in the middle of the night. As I write another quick snippet is mentioned on the 9 am news.

Last week a pianist I met at my last ballet performance referred somebody needing a piano player for a wedding reception to me. The fee was £70 for 2 hours so I did it. It seemed to go well.

I'd better get this in the post now. I hope you're getting enough cups of tea!

Love
Alan

Alan has always loved music and longs for a job that would use his talents. I learned to play the piano once, though it was a long time ago now.

1957, East Ham, East London, U.K.

'Come on, Girlie, follow my fingers.' Dad placed my little hands over his big, railway hands. We laughed as we played *Three Blind Mice*.

'This note here is very important. It's your *middle C*. The notes have the names of the letters in the alphabet, *A, B, C, D, E, F, G* and then it starts again at *A*.'

Every evening, I dragged Dad into the freezing front room to teach me short pieces of piano music, first learning the right hand, then the left hand, and finally both hands together under the black-beaded eyes of a china dog that sat on top of the piano.

I loved my piano lessons. It was nice feeling close to Dad, and Mum couldn't touch me when I was with him.

'How old were you when you learned to play the piano, Dad?'

'Your Nanna sent me for lessons when I was eight, same age as you. I had to go to an old lady's house. She was very strict. She used to place pennies on the backs of your hands and you had to keep them there while you played. If they fell off, it was *whack* with her ruler.'

The months passed and we came to the end of *Pianoforte Primer for Children.*

'That's good, Girlie, you're coming along a treat. Won't be long now and you'll be able to take your first piano exam. I'll put you in for your Trinity College Grade One.'

His words made me feel warm inside, like drinking a mug of hot cocoa on a cold day.

Monday 10th August 1992, Kabul, Afghanistan.

'Today there are attacks from three directions against the government forces...There is not enough medicine in the hospitals...' Mr Rasheed is conveying the BBC Pashto news to me in English.

'Three directions? Is that one group on three sides or three separate groups?'

Mr Rasheed speaks to his sisters, they go to the kitchen and return with a large silver serving plate and seven glasses.

Mr Rasheed places the silver platter on the floor. 'Look, this plate is Kabul.'

He places a glass on the rim of the plate. *'Jamiat-e Islami-e-Afghanistan.'*

'In English?'

'The Islamic Society of Afghanistan. Their leader is Burhanuddin Rabbani and their military commander is Ahmad Shah Massoud.'

Mr Rasheed places a second glass next to the first. 'Now, here is *Shura-e Nazar,* that means Supervisory Council. It's a federation of military forces led by various Mujahedin commanders, mostly from the north and northeast of Afghanistan. They are also led by Massoud.'

'So Massoud is commanding two militias?'

Mr Rasheed points to the two glasses. 'Exactly. They are up here on the hills. Rabbani and Massoud studied together at Kabul University. They became involved in the Afghan resistance against Russia. Massoud was our hero then. We called him "the Lion of Panjshir". He ambushed the Russians in the Salang tunnel. His men waited until a Russian convoy entered the tunnel. Then they exploded the exit. As the Russians ran back out of the entrance, his fighters shot them down. Nowadays they are supported by Tajikistan.'

I can see Mr Rasheed's face light up as he tells the story of Massoud's simple tactics overcoming the Russian military Goliath.

'The *Jamiat* leader, Rabbani, was taking his turn as President when Hekmatyar attacked to remove him from power and take over.'

This is getting complicated. I rummage through my handbag and extract my notebook and pen.

'Heckmatyar?' I question.

Mr Rasheed placed a third glass on the opposite side of the plate. '*Hezb-e Islami*, meaning Islamic party, they are Pashtuns. Their leader is Gulbuddin Hekmatyar. He also attended Kabul University. He is a strong leader because he is supported by Pakistan and America.'

'He's the one who is sending his rockets over today?'

'Exactly, and you should write this down too. When the Russians withdrew from Afghanistan, they made their own man, Najibullah, President of Afghanistan. He's hiding somewhere under the protection of the United Nations. Officers in his government were too ashamed to work with a Russian collaborator and left to join the Mujahedeen. That was the Afghan resistance under the Russian occupation. The resistance was not just one militia, it was many groups. They formed a coalition, taking turns to have their leader as president. Heckmatyar refused to participate. He wanted all the power to himself. Others followed his example and now everyone is fighting each other.'

'So, we've got these two, Rabbani and Massoud... here... supported by Tajikistan, and Rabbani was taking his turn as president when Heckmatyar... here..., supported by Pakistan and America, tried to seize power.'

'Exactly, but let me continue.'

He places the fourth glass on the top rim of the plate. *'Janbish-e Milli-e Islami-e Afghanistan.* That's the National Front. They are based in northern Afghanistan. Their leader is Colonel Rashid Dostum. He was a general in the Soviet-backed Afghan army during the 1980s. He mutinied and formed his own militia. He is a strong leader. He has scud missiles. He is supported by Uzbekistan and Turkmenistan.'

I don't know what scud missiles are. In this case, I think ignorance is the better option.

Mr Rasheed places the fifth glass on the rim of the silver platter. 'This is *Hizb-e Wahdat-e Islami-e Afghanistan,* The Islamic Unity Party of Afghanistan, they are Hazara Shias. Their leader is Abdul Ali Mazari. They are supported by Iran.'

'So that... is Dostum in the north, supported by Uzbekistan and Turkmenistan and that... is Mazari, supported by Iran.'

I'm already struggling to understand the plot and I can see there are still two glasses left.

'This is *Ittihad-i Islami Bara-ee Azadi Afghanistan.* That's the Islamic Union for the Freedom of Afghanistan. *Ittihad* is Pashtun, headed by Abdul Rabb al-Rasul Sayyaf. They are supported by Saudi Arabia. Lastly, we have *Harakat-e Islami-yi Afghanistan,* Islamic Movement of Afghanistan, a Shi'a faction headed by Mohammad Asef Mohseni and Hossein Anwari, supported by Iran.'

'Iran is behind two or three parties?'

'At least.'

I look at the silver platter with the seven glasses arranged clock-like around its rim.

'All fighting each other at the same time?'

'Exactly. Sometimes one will make an alliance with another, then the alliance will break and they'll fight each other again.'

I point to the centre of the 'clock'. 'And we are in the middle, here?'

'Exactly.'

There's quite a commotion going on outside, a continuous roar of thundering booms punctuated by shattering explosions. Hekmatyar is sending his rockets over in volleys, uncountable numbers in wave after wave of destruction.

'So we are caught in the crossfire between all these groups?'

'Maybe.'

'Maybe? What else could it be?'

'They are deliberately targeting the city. They believe that by destroying Kabul and killing its people, we will admire them for it and support them.'

'A multitude of factions, I can just about take in. Trying to win support by killing the people whose allegiance they hope to win? I don't understand that at all. I guess the fighting centres on Kabul because it's the capital. He who has Kabul has Afghanistan.'

'Yes. One day one of them will win but all he will have will be a graveyard.'

'You said they have support from other countries, America, Saudi Arabia, Pakistan. Why do other countries support them?'

'Most of them are our neighbours. They would like to annex Afghanistan to extend their territories.'

'And the others? America, Saudi?'

'Oil and gas! Whoever controls Afghanistan, controls a cheap and easy route to pipe oil and gas from the Caspian Sea to the West.'

'*Ah*, I'm beginning to see. That's why America supported the Afghan resistance under the Russian occupation. It wants to lay its oil and gas pipeline through Afghanistan. It can't do that if...'

'...if someone not politically sympathetic to America wins. Exactly.'

Then comes a deep, sinister boom from some distance away.

I look at Mr Rasheed. 'Is that a bomb?'

Mr Rasheed is silent. The atmosphere in the corridor changes from nervous to tense. I've kind of adjusted to rockets, artillery, gunfire. This is a deeper, darker thundering bringing a deeper, darker foreboding. We hear the blasts of three further bombs, mercifully for us some distance away. We sit silently, each of us inside our own unspoken world, contemplating this new and terrifying turn of events.

I have a problem to solve and who better to advise me than Mr Rasheed? I admire his intellect, his understanding of the complexities of the war and his business mind.

'Mr Rasheed, I'm wondering about moving the Oxfam office to somewhere where it's easier to work, just for a month or so, until the situation here settles down.'

I study Mr Rasheed's reaction. He's an experienced businessman and doesn't betray his thoughts.

'I'm wondering where to. Peshawar's safe but we'd be working across the border and it's frequently closed. There's already an Oxfam office in Panjao but they're so remote they depend on us to keep them supplied. There's another Oxfam office in Phul-i-Khumri but the town doesn't have the banking and trading facilities we need.'

Mr Rasheed thinks for a moment. 'Mazar-i-Sharif. There are banking and money-changing facilities, flights between

Islamabad, Mazar and Hazarajat for Panjao and an escape route via Uzbekistan in case you need it.'

'How safe is it?'

'Much safer than Kabul. It's General Dostum's area. He's a strong commander which means he is rarely attacked. He pays his militia a small salary and they wear a uniform of brown tunics. This makes it easier for him to control them, so there's not the looting that we get here in Kabul. He's quite liberal. Women can go out unveiled, girls go to school and women to university. There are even cinemas where you can watch Hindi films! You and your staff will be much safer there.'

That's it, then. Decided. Mazar-i-Sharif it will be, just for a month or two, to continue operations until things quieten down in Kabul.

That evening there is chaos. One of the factions declares victory and his fighters go crazy. There's a frenzy of gunfire, and bullets rain down on the roof like giant hailstones so heavily that we can't hear each other speak above the din. It's the most terrifying experience of my life. From deep within my subconscious mind, some primeval instinct asserts itself. My body freezes. I cannot move. As in a bad dream, I try to move my left foot. It stays still. I attempt to make my right hand clench into a fist. It refuses to respond. I sit in petrified immobility until the gunfire begins to slow and my instinct abates, releasing my body from its grip.

CHAPTER 10: EVACUATION

Tuesday 11th August, Kabul, Afghanistan

This morning there's a lull. With the promise to return before dark, I leave the Rasheed house. I walk quickly, keeping close to the pock-marked wall. I have to make contact with Islamabad and ask them to pass a message to Michael telling him what I'm doing. Then I'll just have to get into Suzie with any of the staff who are willing to come and drive. I hope Zia will come. Otherwise, it will be down to me to talk my way past the groups of gunmen roaming the streets and that option doesn't appeal to me, not one little bit.

I unlock the office door. Luckily, nobody has been in. Even better, there is water left in the tank on the roof. I take a shower and change the clothes I've been wearing for the last two days and nights.

I go to the radio. The windows have been blown open. There are holes in the mosquito screening and splinters of shrapnel on the table where the radio stands. I pick up two shards of the twisted metal fragments. Perhaps they'll bring me luck. I drop them into my handbag.

The electricity is off and the radio battery is running low. I hope there's enough charge left to call up Islamabad.

'Alpha India, Alpha India, this is Juliet Kilo,' I repeat until the radio sparks into life. They know who and where I am.

This time I'm lucky. Michael is in the U.N. office. His distinctive Irish accent sounds on the radio.

'Hi, it's Michael. What's the *weather* like there? Over.'

'Very bad. We are unable to continue operations. We need to move to *Mike* location as soon as possible in order to maintain the programme until the *weather* improves here. Over.'

Michael will understand that *Mike* is the call sign for Mazar-i-Sharif. I hope the Mujahedeen, who can hear our conversation on looted radios, are less well informed.

'Where are Zia and Nafisa? Over.'

'They have not been able to come because of the *weather*. I am alone here. Over.'

'But the guards, they are there, aren't they? Over.'

I don't want to say that Samimi and Babur have gone. An unguarded office invites intrusion.

'I am alone here. The *weather* is very bad. The radio battery needs recharging but the power is out. We are moving to Mike location as soon as possible. Over.'

It's as much information as I dare to broadcast. The ending of the call cuts my connection with the outside world. I'm utterly, totally alone.

Wednesday 12th August, Kabul, Afghanistan

It's much quieter today with only the odd roll of thunder-like booms. Zia has made it to the office and brought Ehsan, Musa and Nafisa in Suzie.

'Mrs Eileen, Gulshad is sorry she cannot come,' says Zia. 'Her home has suffered worse damage. She must to stay at brother's home with her children and he does not allow her to go out of house.'

I lead them to some chairs around a table and Musa brings a kettle of tea.

'I'm glad to see you are all safe and well.'

There are nods and murmurs of *'Allah be praised'*.

'I'd like to work from Mazar-i-Sharif for a month or two and then see how things are for coming back to Kabul. I understand you want to be with your families but would any of you consider going to Mazar-i-Sharif to help in the new office?'

There's a discussion in rapid Dari.

Nafisa speaks, 'We all will come. We will be safer in Mazar-i-Sharif.'

'That's very kind,' I reply, 'but there isn't room in the little Suzuki for all of us plus the office books and equipment.'

Another discussion, then Zia speaks for them. 'I will come, I can drive and get us through city. I have the cousins in Mazar-i-Sharif who will help us find offices. Nafisa will come also in Suzuki. She also has cousin in Mazar-i-Sharif and can live there. Others will come later with families.'

It's a great relief that Zia is willing to come. In Afghanistan everything that matters works on a system of personal networks and reciprocal favours. Zia's web of contacts appears limitless. He seems to have a relative or acquaintance in every government department, remote village and war-torn city centre marketplace. I'll need him, his connections and his negotiating skills if I'm to do any meaningful work in Mazar-i-Sharif.

I can see Musa is disappointed. 'Musa, I need you to stay with your family. When it's safe to leave your house, please come and check the office is secure.'

Nafisa grins. 'He is saying, "I will stay here. I will protect the office with my life. If you come back and find the office is destroyed, you will find my dead body still guarding the entrance."'

This is not the reaction I am expecting. 'Oh, no, Musa. There is no need for you to die. Just come when it is safe to leave your house.'

I want to make provision for staff wages during our absence from Kabul. Due to the prolonged closure of the banks, there isn't enough money left to pay everyone their full salary. I ask Zia and Nafisa, as the senior staff, to decide how to allocate what cash we have. This is not because I want to abdicate my responsibility. If I were to distribute shares according to my western notions of fairness there would simply be a later 'redistribution' when I'm not there to see it. I prefer to know now.

After a rapid discussion in Dari, Nafisa looks up at me. 'Eileen, we have decided Ehsan, Musa and Gulshad will receive all of their wages because they have need for their families. Zia and I will wait until there is money.'

'That's a good decision,' I reply.

Nafisa bristles, inferring the unintended criticism that they were able to make a bad choice.

'It is the custom of Afghan people to help the poor,' she says sharply.

'What about the guards, Samimi and Babur?' I ask.

'No,' replies Nafisa, 'they deserted and have not returned. They have no honour. They do not deserve.'

'I just don't want any repercussions,' I reply, 'I think we should give each of them a share of the money, thank them politely and tell them we don't need them any longer because we are leaving Kabul. Perhaps that way they will feel they have left with honour. Otherwise they might retaliate against the office or the staff left in Kabul.'

Nafisa glares her disapproval.

Zia nods his agreement. 'Yes, I think you are right. Once before, Mr Michael told me to dismiss someone and I did it. Then one day he stood with his brothers outside my house with machine gun, demanding that I come out and they will kill me.'

'Yes,' says Nafisa, 'and Ehsan had to go to the Mujahedeen commander and beg him to come to stop them killing Zia. I was too much afraid for Zia's life.'

'OK, then,' I say, 'let's pay Samimi, Babur, Ehsan, Musa and Gulshad. I'll make sure you both receive your salaries as soon as we can.'

Zia says, 'Food is expensive now and Gulshad has not enough for her children. We should give her food from emergency cupboard.'

Nafisa draws me aside. 'Eileen, Gulshad is a widow, she has eight children, she cannot come even to this office and certainly not Mazar-i-Sharif. Ehsan is Hazara, there are men who will kill him if they see his face. It is for him too much dangerous. He cannot travel. Musa is old, he needs his family to care for him. I must come. Without this work, my family will make me stay in the house and never leave it. I will go crazy.'

I understand Nafisa's desire to come. Will her father allow it?

An hour later Jolyon comes to the office. 'Michael said you are going to Mazar-i-Sharif. We're going on Thursday and he asked me to take you along with us. There's one space left in the cars. Do you want to come?'

Zia speaks up, 'Mrs Eileen, we will need Suzuki to work in Mazar-i-Sharif. You must go with Mr Jolyon. We will go by Suzuki.'

'I don't like to go with the convoy while you and Nafisa risk going by yourselves. I shall come with you in the Suzuki.'

Zia and Nafisa look at each other in alarm.

'No,' says Zia, 'is impossible. It is dangerous if you are with us. Without you we will say we are the husband and wife and no-one will question us. We will be only another couple leaving city.'

In the absence of any better suggestions, I reluctantly agree.

The plan is to leave at dawn the next morning. To ensure a quick getaway, Zia will spend the night in the office while Nafisah and I stay with Mr Rasheed next door. Zia, Ehsan and Nafisa go home in the Suzuki. Zia and Nafisa will tell their families what's happening and bring their bags back to the office ready for the morning. I go to the door to see them off.

Hours are ticking by. I'm worried. Why is it taking them so long to return? Has there been another tragedy? What shall I do if they don't return?

I hear the Suzuki draw into the compound and rush outside. Nafisa is trembling. Her mascara is smudged, her eyes are red. Zia's face is taut. Nafisa sobs on my shoulder as I lead her inside. Over a cup of tea, she tells me that a Mujahedeen gang requisitioned the Suzuki. At gunpoint, they forced Zia to put a mutilated body into the pick-up and drive the bloody cargo to the dead man's home on the other side of the city.

Zia spends an hour hosing and scrubbing the blood from the floor of the Suzuki while Nafisa is calming down.

'Nafisa, what did your father say when you asked if you could go to Mazar-i-Sharif?'

'He placed the Holy Qur'an on my head and blessed me. He said I must go and be safe.'

At 4:30 pm Zia squeezes the last milliamp of charge from the radio and calls the U.N. in Islamabad asking them to inform the Oxfam office of our imminent departure. Then, while there is still daylight, he disconnects the radio for the journey, shutting down our final lifeline to the outside world. So I don't hear the exchange between Jolyon and the head of security as they discuss 'Operation Breakfast,' the code name for the evacuation.

'Breakfast is off, I repeat, breakfast is off. Over.'

'Breakfast is on. I will go ahead as planned,' Jolyon replies.

'No, you are traumatised from recent events and it's affecting your decisions. It's far too dangerous. It's suicidal. Wait until things are quieter and we can arrange it properly. Over.'

'Breakfast is on. Over and out.'

For the next task, Zia brings a ladder. 'We should get Samimi and Babur's weapons down and send message to them to come and collect.'

I don't know how the guns will be returned to the guards, nor how they will receive their wages and the message that we are leaving Kabul. I assume that Zia's web of contacts will deal with it.

The evacuation is a strictly a 'one bag and a bottle of water' job. There's little office packing to do since the Mujahedeen relieved Oxfam of most of its possessions shortly before I arrived a month ago. I put the codan radio and office laptop into my bag. Zia and Nafisa can't risk bringing anything other than some personal possessions in the Suzuki, nothing that looks any different from the thousands of others leaving Kabul. I pack my own belongings into my two suitcases and leave them at Mr Rasheed's house. I wear my money and passport in their usual place, a pocket sewn into my underwear – the passport so they can identify my body and the dollars so I can pay my own ransom.

Thursday 13th August, Kabul, Afghanistan

The city has been under fire since 4:30 this morning. At 7 am, Zia and Nafisa drop me off at the meeting point, the UNOCA Staff House and then start their journey out of Kabul.

Jolyon Leslie and John Tacon, the leaders of this expedition, declare it too dangerous for us to leave. Together with a small group of residents of the staff house, I wait behind a wall of sandbags, watching flames consume the TV station in the near distance, the smoke rising in a straight column in the windless air.

'I've a message for Eileen Masters,' calls out Jolyon.

I catch his eye.

'I've a message from your boss, Michael. He sends you best wishes for your journey. Please radio him when you arrive and he wants you to count the number of people leaving Kabul.'

A trickle of laughter greets this last request.

Count them? How on earth am I supposed to do that?

At about ten in the morning, John and Jolyon decide it's time to go. To the sound of shelling and rocket fire, three vehicles make their way along the streets of Kabul. Gangs of armed men are hunting in packs for the spoils of war. Thousands are escaping. A woman struggles to keep hold of her child's hand from under an all-enveloping *burqa*. A man and a woman push a handcart containing their belongings, their children perched on top. A man carries an old lady on his back.

Jolyon is driving the first Landcruiser immediately behind the armed escort vehicle. He seems to know everyone in Kabul. He greets every gunman who stops us as a long-standing friend with an Afghan right-fist-on-heart salute and a generous handshake.

John Tacon drives the second vehicle. I'm in the front passenger seat with my handbag tucked between my feet. There's a couple I don't know in the back. Above us, rockets and artillery shells are ripping the sky apart. I ought to be scared but if this little convoy were to be hit, there's absolutely nothing I can do about it, so what's the point of being anxious? I sit back and watch the blue U.N. flag flutter on the front of the vehicle as Kabul speeds past us.

1958, East Ham, London, U.K.

I was nine years old, running away from home, hurrying toward my grandmother's house. I had to get away, stop it happening again. It had started as soon as I'd got home from school.

I reached for the latch key round my neck but Mum opened the door and ushered me in with a flick of her head.

'I've been stuck indoors all day with one of my heads. Put your old clothes on and come down soon as you're washed, I need you to peel veg.'

'But Mum, I want to practise my scales before Dad gets home. I need...'

'You need? It's always what little Miss Perfect needs these days, isn't it? Get on with it. You can play around at the piano later, when your Dad gets home.'

I came downstairs in my old clothes and went into the kitchen. I sighed wearily.

'I'm in no mood for your amateur dramatics, girl. I've done a meat pie. Get spuds and carrots from the larder, wash 'n' peel, you know what's what.'

'How many, Mum?'

'How many, Mum?' she repeated, mocking my higher-pitched tone. 'Well there's six of us. How many do you think, Miss Brain of Britain? I thought you were top of the class for sums, or was the last school report a pack of lies?'

'OK, I'll get enough.'

I darted into the larder and wrestled six decent-sized spuds from the sack, cut into quarters that'd make four each, plus a handful of carrots and ran some water into the bowl.

Mum frowned and rubbed her forehead. 'Cold tap, hot tap costs money. That's our bath water you're wasting.'

I washed and scraped away at the potatoes and carrots then dropped them into pans of water.

'Can I practise my scales now, Mum?'

'No, young lady, you can't. Kathleen very kindly spilt milk on her frock today. It needs soaking in Lux and a decent scrubbing. I can't do anything with this damn head.'

I let slip a tiny noise, a stifled *huh*. Mum caught onto it like Peter the cat leaping onto a mouse.

'What was that?'

'Nothing.'

'Don't lie to me girl, don't you start lying again.' She dragged me out of the kitchen and into the hall. I wriggled to release myself from her grip.

My three younger sisters, Kathleen, Mary and Christine, scurried terrified up the stairs and peered down at me through the banister rails.

'I'm not lying, I didn't say a word.'

In one long-armed swoop, Mum whacked me across the side of the head, opened the door to the cupboard under the stairs and threw me inside. She slammed the door shut, sealing me into the darkness, among the shoes, the Hoover and old coats. Everything smelled stale. It was difficult to breathe.

'Let me out!'

'You think you can make fun of me? I'd like to see you cook and clean and run a house full of girls, all messing the place up. You can stay in there until you suffocate, that'll shut you up!'

I hammered on the door for a while and then gave up. I pushed down my panic like putting a lid on a steaming saucepan. I had an idea. *She wants me to suffocate. OK, I'll teach her.* I stood in total silence. I closed my eyes, imagined I was among the sunflowers, swallowed the urge to scream.

'I'm going to put you in the children's home, then you'll have to do as you're told.'

I remained motionless and mute.

Her curiosity or maybe her fear overcame her. She opened the cupboard door and peered inside. I rushed out past her, through the hall to the front door and out along the road.

It was cold and I didn't have my coat. The streetlights came on. I still had so far to go. The bus looked warm, well-lit and safe, but I didn't have the fare.

Thursday 13th August 1992, on the road to Mazar-i-Sharif, Afghanistan

Beyond Kabul the road clears, then the cars stop. Jolyon pays off the armed escort and with a lot of handshaking and thanks, dismisses them to return to their homes.

The journey continues.

John reaches down to tune the two-way car radio to the U.N. frequency.

A voice calls.

'Tango mobile, what is your location, please? Over.'

John replies, 'On the outskirts of Kilo location. Over.'

'Any problems? Over.'

'Negative, no probs at all. Over.'

'OK. We're monitoring you all the way. Good luck. Over and out.'

'Thanks. Over and out.'

It's comforting to know that we are not entirely alone, that there are people who are sharing our perilous journey, even though they are many miles away.

The two cars travel through the Selang Pass. We stop for a short break.

'Don't wander off, anyone,' Jolyon calls out, 'there are landmines around.'

After a short break we resume our travel through the heart of the Hindu Kush Mountains. I sit back and enjoy the ride through the spectacular alpine scenery along the mountain pass, watching the river trickling alongside. *You'd pay a lot of money for a trip like this anywhere else in the world.*

I haven't brought food for the journey. I didn't think of it in the whirl of preparing the office for our absence. The couple in the back, whose names I don't know, produce a large bag. They take out a packet of savoury crackers, paste butter and paté onto each one and pass them round.

'Do have some, we've brought plenty for everyone.'

Somehow, as the car jumps and jerks over the bumpy road, they manage to pour lemonade into four cups without spilling any.

'Would you like some more? There's loads in the bag.'

It's been a long time since breakfast and the impromptu picnic goes down rather well. Whoever you are, thank you for bringing and sharing it.

John picks up a conversation on the radio. 'That's your boss,' he says, passing the microphone to me. 'You can talk to him.'

I wait until Michael finishes his conversation with the Panjao office.

'Alpha India, this is Juliet mobile. Over.'

'Hi, Eileen, where are you? Over.'

I don't have a clue. I look queryingly at John. He laughs and tells me some unpronounceable name that I try to repeat into the radio microphone.

'We've been following you on the radio. What's your E.T.A.? Over.'

This time John supplies the answer without waiting for the querying look and I repeat it.

'E.T.A. 1700 hours. Please can you contact my husband, Alan, and tell him we're OK? Over.'

'Will do. Contact me as soon as you reach your destination. Over.'

'Have to get someone to connect up the radio first but will do my best. Over'

'OK. Good luck. Over and out.'

'Over and out.'

Thursday 13ᵗʰ August 1992, Islamabad, Pakistan

Dear Alan,

I have just spoken to Eileen on the radio. As planned, she left Kabul today by road with Oxfam staff and other people from the UN. The road is excellent and they were mobile when I talked to her. They are setting up office in Mazar and I hope to fly out to see them in a week or so.

Best regards. Michael Semple

1958, East Ham, London, U.K.

My grandmother sat me on her lap, wrapping her warm arms around me.

'It's alright, dear. Granddad will go and tell Mummy and Daddy you're here. We'll sort out everything else in the morning.'

Thursday 13th August 1992, Mazar-i-Sharif, Afghanistan

A full ten hours of travelling have passed when the two Landcruisers enter the Staff House compound in Mazar-i-Sharif. I'm shown upstairs to a room. It's clean and comfortable. My head still thinks it's travelling. I already wish I'd brought my travel jug to make a cup of tea. I'll get one later from the canteen downstairs.

There's a tap at the door and the receptionist peers in.

'There are some people here to see you. They don't have security clearance to come in.'

I rush down to the gate.

Zia grins. 'Nice place you have here!'

I greet Nafisa with the traditional two-way kiss and we linger in a hug. Then I defy the culture to shake Zia's hand.

'Where are you staying tonight?' I ask.

'We both have cousins nearby,' Zia replies. 'I will drop Nafisa and bring Suzuki back. It will be safer here for night.'

Tomorrow, we shall have work to do. For now, it's enough that we are all safe and that the warm night air holds nothing more than the precious sounds of peace.

CHAPTER 11: BUSINESS AS USUAL

Friday 14th August, Mazar-i-Sharif, Afghanistan

I wake to the sound of dawn prayers from the mosque. After breakfast, I return to my room. I'm restless. I want to get on with finding an office but it's Friday, the traditional Afghan day off and frustratingly, I know I won't be able to do much today. I plug in the laptop and start typing:

FIELD OFFICE REPORT

Evacuation of Kabul Office

By the end of the morning, the report is nine pages long.

Saturday 15th August 1992, Mazar-i-Sharif, Afghanistan

The U.N. Staff House fills to the brim with waves of aid workers coming from Kabul. The space is needed for U.N. personnel and I have to find somewhere else to stay.

John Tacon kindly offers to let me stay at his house. 'Ann and I will be away this weekend. Make yourself at home. Jolyon here will show you where it is,' he adds with a grin.

I hang around in the canteen for a while, not sure what to do. Jolyon is busy organising this and that, sending people here and there. When everyone has gone and the canteen is quiet, he turns to me.

'Take your vehicle and follow me,' he says with that confident air that radiates from natural leaders.

I remember my clumsy attempts to drive Suzi in Kabul and contemplate saying, 'Actually, I don't drive,' but that doesn't feel like a possible option at the moment. I'm in a man's world and playing the feeble female, well, it just doesn't fit the bill.

With no room to turn the Suzuki around, my first manoeuvre is to reverse out of the gates, over an open gully and onto the road. I look in the rear view mirror. I can't see a thing because of the tarpaulin cover that is hooped over the back. I look in the wing mirrors. It doesn't help much. Suzi jerks backwards.

'Don't you let me down, Suzie,' I say aloud.

Keeping my feet firmly where they are, I'm slowly reversing. I hope I'm going toward the gates, not the guards standing by it.

'Come on, Suzie, we can do it.'

The gates emerge from behind Suzie and pass along her sides until they stand in front of me. I turn the steering wheel. Reversing onto the road, I feel a wheel drop into the roadside gully. I stop and take a deep breath. Jolyon's vehicle is in front, waiting for me. I lift the gear stick into first and we lurch forward. Jolyon speeds off. A few yards behind him, Suzie skips along the road trying to keep up.

So here I am, grateful to John and Ann for the use of their house, but wishing I knew my way around better so I could find an office. If this were Sukkur or Murree in Pakistan, I'd know what to do. My knowledge of Mazar-i-Sharif just isn't up to it and my Dari is totally inadequate for following up the leads, negotiating the terms. Perhaps if I go back to the Staff House I could find someone who...

There's a knock at the door.

'Mrs Eileen, there is office. I need $100 to pay landlord. We must be quick, before someone will offer more.'

Zia sounds quite out of breath as if he's been hurrying. I quickly take the amount he asks for from my handbag and he rushes away.

Saturday 15 August 1992, Mazar-i-Sharif, Afghanistan

Hello everyone,

We evacuated the Kabul office on Thursday, having been under heavy fire for days. It was a bit dicey getting out of Kabul city with the stuff still coming down and uncontrolled gangs but we made it in the U.N. convoy. Once out of Kabul it was a very easy journey.

This morning we rented some rooms in a house to use as an office and my accommodation. It's adequate and we can move in tomorrow.

I'm writing this hoping to find someone who is travelling. There's no post as flights are suspended because the airport keeps coming under fire.

Before we left Kabul, some shrapnel from an exploding rocket came through my office window. I have kept some bits as a souvenir.

Write soon.

Eileen/00Mum

Sunday 16th August 1992, Mazar-i-Sharif, Afghanistan

Today, two rooms become the Oxfam office. Nafisa and I dust and clean while Zia fixes up the codan radio. The rooms come complete with red sleeping mats. That's useful because I'm going to be sleeping on the floor.

'Eileen, please let me stay here with you,' pleads Nafisa, 'my cousin's house has too many people and I don't like it there.'

'OK, Nafisa, there's space for both of us.'

Nafisa's eyes glow with delight.

We have water from an outside tap. The toilet is a hole in the garden with roughly-built brick walls and an old sack for a door. The hole leads to the open sewage gully that runs along the side of the road outside. Tomorrow, I'll ask Zia to buy a bucket for flushing the toilet. We don't need furniture since we're only going to be here for a few weeks until things settle down in Kabul. Yes, I'm happy with the progress we've made today.

Monday 17th August 1992, Mazar-i-Sharif, Afghanistan

I'd like to help the people who fled from Kabul, the I.D.P.s, (internally displaced people), who are now living in horrible conditions in every overcrowded room in the city. I'm pleased when Zia brings a *sitor* from Michael instructing us to do just that.

'But first, we must see Provincial Governor for permission to enter the camps and interview people,' says Zia.

The office of the Provincial Governor is packed with people who just seem to be waiting for something to happen. The Governor spots my white face and signals to me to approach. Zia and Nafisa accompany me to his desk.

'Come, sit beside me. What is your name?'

'Eileen Masters.'

'You are beautiful.'

'Thank you. We've come to ask for a permit to enter the schools and camps where displaced people are being accommodated.'

'Your eyes are blue. They are pretty. Come, sit closer to me.'

Oh dear. Well, if it gets us the permit... I slide my chair closer to his.

'We'd like to interview them, find out what they need, please, if you will give us permission?'

'That's a pretty colour. Pink suits you. You have a husband?'

'Yes.'

'Where is he?'

'He's... just... I think... over there in that office,' I fib.

I hear Nafisa stifle a giggle.

'If you could grant us a permit in the name of Oxfam, we would be able to help supply a few essentials to the people in the schools and camps.'

'Are you sure you have a husband? It seems strange that you come here alone if you have a husband. If you were my wife, I would take better care of you.'

He's leaning toward me, a bit too closely for my comfort but I need to get that permit.

'Sir, if you could see your way to granting us the necessary documents, you would make me very happy.'

'I will give you the permit if you will promise to come again and see me. Next time we will take tea together.'

I force a smile. 'Of course.'

Anything for those wretched papers.

The Governor signals with his chin to a man standing beside him. The man disappears momentarily and returns with a fistful of forms and a rubber stamp.

Back in the safety of the Suzuki, Zia and Nafisa explode with laughter.

'He likes you too much, Eileen,' giggles Nafisa.

'We got the papers, didn't we? Come on, we've work to do.'

Tuesday 18th August 1992, Mazar-i-Sharif, Afghanistan

A long crocodile of people waits by the school gates, ushered back by a few armed police as the Suzuki approaches. Nafisa and I wait while Zia chats with the guards. He shows them our permit from the Provincial Governor. The guards open the gates and we drive through.

'He knows my cousin very well,' explains Zia, 'he says school is full now, they don't know where to put those who still are arriving.'

Nafisa and I follow Zia through the mass of people packed kettle-tight inside the corridor. Anxious faces peer at us.

A man asks Zia when help will arrive. 'The government food ration is not enough and we have no money. Give us money so that we can buy what our families need.'

Zia smiles. 'Help is nearby, on its way soon.'

He chats to an older man who appears to be the spokesman for three families from Kabul.

'When the shelling stopped, the city went silent at first. Then gunfire lit up the sky. Men appeared, roaming the streets, looting and opening fire on anything that moved – old men, women, young children. My office was destroyed and I have no job. Then rockets destroyed my house.'

A younger man joins the conversation. 'We hired a truck to take us home to Kabul from Quetta because we believed the fighting was over but we couldn't enter the city because of the shelling. We camped where we were for several days. Then we came to Mazar-i-Sharif. We have spent all our money getting here. Even if the fighting stops we cannot afford to return to Kabul.'

Zia stays to talk to the men. Nafisa and I move toward a group of women.

A woman grips my arm, sobbing. 'My husband and sons went off to fight and I don't know where they are, or whether they are alive or dead.'

I don't have the words to comfort her.

'Please come,' says another woman. Stepping over other people, she leads us to her family sitting in a close circle on the floor. 'Please help my husband, please!'

A man lying on the filthy floor lifts his long, Afghan shirt and shows us an open wound caused by shrapnel that went into the left side of his chest. How can anyone survive such an injury? I'm amazed how life can be, at the same time, so fragile and so strong.

Nafisa and I sit down on the floor next to some more women.

'We are very grateful for the food but we can't cook it because we don't have stoves or equipment,' says one.

'We need sleeping mats and blankets. We are sleeping on the bare floor with nothing to cover us,' says another.

A woman leans toward us and whispers, 'Please, make a place for us to wash ourselves and our sanitary cloths. Here, there's nowhere and it's embarrassing. The men go to the mosque to wash, we can't.'

'We need soap,' says another. 'We are wearing the same clothes we wore when we fled Kabul eight days ago. And condoms, we need condoms, the last thing we need is to get pregnant now.'

At the end of the corridor, downcast faces are wrapped in clothing, noses shielded from the stench coming from the toilets. I glance quickly inside the facility. A toilet block designed for schoolchildren to use once or twice a day, has become a stinking well of potential disease.

Back at the office, I send a short message to Islamabad.

Urgent. Please move heaven and earth to get a sanitation engineer out here as soon as.

Oh that life were that simple. Frustratingly, the reply I eventually get back is: *He can't come. He's in Somalia working on the famine.*

Thursday 20th August 1992, Mazar-i-Sharif, Afghanistan

It's a week today since our evacuation. The intensity of the situation in Kabul was such that we all are showing signs of trauma – aches in our limbs, loss of appetite and an inability to concentrate.

Nafisa frequently talks about the experiences of being under fire in Kabul and of the journey. Zia has become even more withdrawn. I sense that he is irritated by Nafisa's 'rocket stories'.

Nafisa puts her scarf over her head. 'Are you coming Eileen?'

'Coming where?'

'To the mosque, to wail for our loss.'

'No, thank you, Nafisa. It's not our custom and I wouldn't know what to do.'

Zia's eyes show concern. 'Oh, you must, Mrs Eileen, or you will go crazy.'

They mean well. It's not what I feel I need to do right now. I stay behind while they go to the mosque. *Was Zia right? Should I have gone with them?*

It's quiet in Mazar-i-Sharif, no shelling, no gunfire, just people, bicycles, handcarts and the occasional car or truck breaking the quietness. Impromptu markets have sprung up with penniless people, displaced from Kabul, slowly selling off their meagre possessions one by one, or bartering them for food.

The ringing noise in my ears is taking a while to abate. Zia is having flashbacks. His hobby is painting. I ask him to paint a picture of the scene recurring in his flashbacks. He creates an impressionist-style picture of Kabul in grey tones with red flames rising from the buildings and the people trying to escape the city with as many belongings as they could carry, one man carrying his mother on his back.

Nafisa is also having hearing problems. I joke about us having to shout at each other but I'm worried. Nafisa is obsessively cleaning the Suzuki over and over again, as if she can still see blood on the now spotlessly clean floor of the vehicle.

Friday 21st August 1992, Oxford, U.K.

Dear Eileen,

You survived the rocket attacks, then! They must have come a little too close for comfort. Were the offices themselves damaged? Michael Semple faxed me at work shortly after I phoned to tell me you were all safely on your way to Mazar. For some reason, County Industries didn't think to send it on to me (I'm just completing my second week's holiday) for 3 or 4 days and even then sent it by 2nd class post!

What is your new accommodation like? Were you able to take everything with you?

I've had the house to myself all this last week. Jon's at Bryony's. Dan and Mandy have been enjoying the first week of their fortnight's holiday at a caravan. They say the weather hasn't been wonderful so far but they've used Dan's dinghy a few times at the beach.

Yesterday evening for fun I walked from Kidlington to Oxford along the canal towpath. It was quite a pleasant and quiet walk and it took 1 hour 50 minutes. I went to Burger King for supper then took a bus home.

David and Dagney came to see me this afternoon. He was dropping hints about wanting you to sort out the accounts of his charity in the Philippines. They are in a mess since being taken over (surprise, surprise). I told them you had your hands full as it is. They send their love.

Bryony has got the 'A' level passes she needed for Bath University.

That's all the news up to date so I'll get this off now.

Be good – as I am being.

Love

Alan

Monday 24th August 1992, Mazar-i-Sharif, Afghanistan

We sit on the floor to count the cash. There are over a thousand Afghanis to £1 sterling. We count out Afghani notes in millions. Whenever possible, Zia will bring a sealed, bank-stamped packet of one million Afghani notes. That makes our counting that bit easier. The cash is destined for the projects in Panjao. They don't have banking or exchange facilities and are dependent on us to supply them with what they need. It starts with a radio call.

'We need medicines, urgently. Our usual order, over.'

Zia, Nafisa and I unlock the dollar cash tin. To make sure there are no mistakes we count it twice. Nafisa writes the withdrawal into the cash book. Zia takes the dollars to the mosque and changes it into Afghani notes. Because the banks are still not fully operational, it has to be the traditional moneychangers. Zia will also buy a metal trunk and a sturdy padlock.

When Zia returns, he, Nafisa and I sit in a circle on the floor, the cash in the centre, and count it into bundles of ten-thousand and then into bundles of one million. We all count aloud as Zia loads the cash into the trunk. Then we lock it. Nafisa labels it as medicine with the address of the Panjao office. At the other end, they will break the padlock open.

'Problem is all flights to Bamyan are suspended,' says Zia. 'Weekly flights are stopped due to security problem. I asked to charter flight. They refused us.'

Without the weekly U.N. flights, we have a major problem transporting cash to the rural projects through hostile territory.

Zia has a suggestion. 'We could hire truck, put money under load of manure. No one will look underneath.'

'But how will we load the money without the truck driver seeing it?' asks Nafisa, 'he will not leave his truck unattended for us to do that. We can send it by ambulance. We can take the stuffing out of the seats and fill them with money instead.'

I wasn't keen on that suggestion. 'But Nafisa, if anyone finds out, no ambulance will be able to travel safely again.'

The next day Zia rushes into the office. 'One special flight is leaving this morning for Bamyan. My cousin says he can get permission for us to send small cargo. I must take trunk now, quickly!'

Tuesday 25th August 1992, Mazar-i-Sharif, Afghanistan

I first meet Nyasha Jeremiah Gunda at the U.N. Staff House in Mazar-i-Sharif. Universally known simply as *Gunda*, he's a young Zambian engineer with a huge personality, smiling and singing his way through his volunteer placement. He rents a house and is sub-letting the individual rooms to make a few extra dollars to send to his wife and children at home.

Gunda offers a recently vacated room to me. 'It's a nice place and you'll be safe there.'

I'm not sure. There are four women working in Mazar-i-Sharif. We've talked about getting a house together but it's difficult to find anywhere. Every nook and cranny of the town is already packed tight with displaced people and rents are high.

Well, I've been camping out in the office for a fortnight now, sleeping on a mat on the floor. I don't mind this rough living. It just seems silly to continue with it when an alternative is being offered.

Nafisa is understanding. 'It's OK Eileen. You take Gunda's room. I would if he offered it to me. I'll go back to my cousin's house.'

'But you don't like it there.'

'If they tell my father I am not there he will worry for me. It's best if I go to their house.'

The room in Gunda's Balkh House is simple and sufficient – a bed, a table and chair, a wardrobe. We all contribute to a kitty for food and the employment of an Afghan cook. The shared bathrooms have plumbed-in water, real showers and western-style toilets - simply, luxury.

Although the Oxfam office is operational, communication remains a problem. In the absence of functioning telephone lines, the main form of communication is the radio. Since the Islamabad office doesn't have its own radio, we have to send

123

messages to the U.N. in Islamabad and ask them to pass them on.

'No, we're too busy,' was the answer we often received.

'We could put *sitors* on a computer disk if that would be easier for you?'

'No, there is too much risk of viruses.'

We repeated this conversation with many agencies.

We're feeling very isolated indeed when I write to Michael to try to persuade him that we need our own *sitor* equipment, or a satellite telephone and fax, or at least a radio in the Oxfam Islamabad office so we can speak directly to him instead of having to rely on the goodwill of agencies. I'm told the budget doesn't stretch that far.

'Eileen! Yours!'

I raise both hands and take a leap into the air. I miss. The ball lands behind me.

In the evenings at Balkh House, the boys like to play volleyball. I enjoy playing, though I mostly miss the ball. We all laugh as Gunda places himself behind me and when the ball flies toward us, he punches it back over the net, attributing the perfectly executed volley to me.

There are Afghan men perched on the garden wall, sitting on their haunches, their rifles between their knees. They start calling out abusive names. I try to ignore it for a while.

The shouts are continuing and I'm getting cross. How dare they? It's only a game of volleyball and we have few opportunities for recreation.

A large stone hits me between the shoulders. My temper snaps. I pick up the rock and run at the men. They are armed, I only have a stone in my hand. To my complete astonishment, they run away.

Gunda is furious. 'Didn't you see they're armed? They could have killed us all! Some people have more courage than sense!'

He's right, of course, but I shall never forget the sight of armed men running away when I stood up to them with nothing more than a stone in my hand.

Wednesday 26th August 1992, Mazar-i-Sharif, Afghanistan

Hello everyone,

I don't know how, when or whether this will reach you but here goes.

On 23rd August I received Alan's letter no.1 dated 27th July, letter no.3 dated 2nd August and letter no.4 dated 9th August. There was no letter no.2, must have got lost somewhere. Perhaps it will turn up later.

We are not far from the Uzbekistan border. I have applied for a visa. If it comes in time, I'd like to visit Termez for a few days for a weekend break and to test communications from there. I am hoping it may be possible to set up a post box so mail can reach us. It would mean travelling frequently but at present we are feeling very isolated indeed. There are still no flights in or out, not even U.N. flights.

Mazar is peaceful at present and much easier to work in than Kabul. We are gradually getting the office functioning, though communication remains our worst problem.

I am making progress in learning Dari. It's different from Urdu though the script is the same, which helps. The most confusing bits are where a Persian word means the opposite of what it means in Urdu. For example, *bey* in Urdu means 'without'. In Persian it means 'with'.

Kabul has been under more or less continuous bombardment since we left. Even when the fighting stops, it will take years of work to make the city habitable again. Most people seem to think it never will be.

I have a video of the rocket attacks in Kabul taken by a couple of U.N. guys. Jon will like it. At one point the cameraman has to hit the floor and you see the camera

125

suddenly descending. How he was able to stand on the roof to take the video when the rest of us were scared stiff in our bunkers, I just don't know. Anyway, I have bought a copy to bring home with me so you can see what it was like.

I am now living in a house that's full of men! It's not too bad considering the situation. I have a decent room and the house has water on tap and western-style bathrooms. There's plenty of food, a volleyball court, table tennis and lots of videos.

I am concerned that Mandy's back is still giving her trouble. Do they know the cause?

I assume Dan is still at the bakery. Is Jon contributing to the household budget?

I have just tried out my Persian and it worked. I asked Musa to buy a toilet roll and he came back with the correct item. It's rough stuff and has to perform the double role of a box of tissues.

Yes, I'm getting lots of tea, usually without milk, with lots of sugar and very weak. During our last week in Kabul we did little else other than drink tea. As the saying goes, 'if in doubt, brew up.'

I was only able to bring one bag to Mazar. I had to leave behind my travel jug. I am rather sorry to be without it. I have bought a vacuum flask and keep it filled with tea from the kitchen. Most of my luggage had to stay in Kabul. I left it with a neighbour. I don't know whether it still exists.

If my visa for Uzbekistan arrives and I get to Termez, I'll post this from there. Otherwise I'll have to wait for someone travelling.

It would be nice to hear from Jon or Dan and Mandy.

Love to all

Eileen/00Mum

Friday 28th August 1992, Mazar-i-Sharif, Afghanistan

The rumour that I'm having an affair with Jeremiah Gunda is very annoying. I'm forty-three, married with two adult sons and my favourite activity is relaxing with a cup of tea. Gunda is an energetic young Zambian, dancing and drinking his way through a posting that will provide him with the funds to assure his future. The notion is so patently ridiculous that I wonder at the capacity of otherwise intelligent people to believe anything they are told.

I guess it was the secret driving lessons that did it. Every evening, Zia parks the Suzuki in Gunda's compound and gives me the keys. In the mornings, I drive the short distance to the office.

I didn't notice Gunda watching from the window that day as I attempted the reverse move out of the compound, across the open gully and jerked along the road. The next morning, he came out and stood by the vehicle.

'You can't drive this thing, can you?'

I winced slightly. 'I can drive, I just don't remember some of the details.'

'When you get back this evening I'll give you a driving lesson.'

So there we were, on a quiet back street as I practised under Gunda's instruction. I drove slowly forward, concentrating on awkwardly changing to second gear. A group of dusty boys jumped up and stood on the back bumper, clinging onto the hooped tarpaulin. I stopped suddenly, then jerked forward. It did the trick. They jumped off and ran away.

Gunda was not impressed. 'What are you doing? You could get shot for that, you'll get us both killed!'

That was the end of the driving lessons. The rumour, however, is now firmly established. The forest fire of gossip is out of control and nothing I can say will quench it. I just have to wait for it to burn itself out.

CHAPTER 12: SOAP AND SLEEPING MATS

Tuesday 1st September 1992, Oxford, U.K.

Dear Eileen,

My mother invited me down to Bournemouth on Friday just gone as it was bank holiday weekend. Jon is still at Bryony's but Dan and Mandy were returning from their caravan holiday on Saturday so I left instructions for them to feed Puss Puss and hamster and I went down on Saturday morning.

I got roped into a cricket match at Mum's church. The minister was on the opposing side and was scoring a lot of runs. However, he hit one ball too high and I caught him out. Unfortunately I wasn't so successful when I went in to bat and I was bowled out before I could score!

Did I tell you Bryony obtained the right passes in her 'A' levels to take up her place at Bath University?

Dan came in from work just now and says he's being laid off at the end of this week. He says his boss is having to let him go in order to employ a master baker instead. He has been assured of a good reference. Dan went straight upstairs and changed into a suit and tie and went off to the Job Centre and employment agencies.

In contrast, when I returned from my fortnight's holiday, I had the result of my four-monthly review and my money has gone up by five pounds per week. The basic stayed the same, the extra was performance-related. I shall be going on day shifts for two weeks soon to do some more training. While I was away, two people were sacked and replaced.

Jon arrived home yesterday evening. He and Dan took Dan's dinghy over to the canal and rowed up and down for a while.

Well, look after yourself and remember to keep your face covered – or don't you have to in Mazar?

Love

Alan, Jon, Dan and Mandy

P.S. Dan now has an electronic Mum (as he calls it) – his visa card. The trouble is he overdid it slightly while on holiday not knowing he was going to be made redundant.

Saturday, 5th September 1992, Mazar-i-Sharif, Afghanistan

The garage-like market stall has red sleeping mats piled high from floor to ceiling. I watch Zia and Nafisa begin the long process of bargaining. We need to replenish our supplies for distributing to the people from Kabul who fled with nothing except the clothes they were wearing.

'Do you have 100?' asks Zia.

'Yes, I have a warehouse near the mosque. I can supply 100.'

'What is your price?'

'What price are you offering?'

'You are the seller, you name your price.'

'It is the buyer's privilege to name the price.'

For several minutes, each party tries to get the other to open the negotiations. Eventually, Zia wins and the stallholder asks for 100,000 Afghanis, about £100 for 100 sleeping mats.

Nafisa jumps in. 'That's ridiculous! 50,000 Afghanis and no more!'

The stallholder laughs. 'No! For 100 mats I can't take any less than 100,000 Afghanis.

Nafisa starts to walk away from the stall. 'These mats are rubbish, we can get better elsewhere.'

'Wait, if you order 200, I can give you a discount. They will cost only 190,000 Afghanis. They are all best quality.'

'The mats are for foreigners,' says Zia, 'for giving to the poor. Give us a good price and you will be doing your religious duty and there will be plenty of repeat orders.'

Zia and Nafisa argue, scoff, cajole and persuade until the price of 135,000 Afghanis for 200 mats is agreed and Zia and the stallholder shake hands to seal the deal.

With a final *huh!* from Nafisa, we move on to the next stall, repeating the process until we have obtained 1,000 sleeping mats at the very best prices and mattresses and soap fill every available space in our office.

It is quite a lesson to watch Zia and Nafisa. I love the way they negotiate prices, always quick to spot any trick the seller may try.

1959, East Ham, London, U.K.

'Now then, Girlie, it's time to get you ready for your eleven-plus exam. Come on, I'll test you.'

Dad and I went into the freezing front room of our new house in Sandford Road, East Ham. Dad had moved up a bit in his job to being a 'Permanent Way Inspector'. That meant, instead of laying and repairing the dock's railway lines, he checked them. We had moved to East Ham, a definite rung up the social ladder from Silvertown and it was nicer than our old house with a bathroom and an indoor toilet. In our previous house, there was no bathroom. We had to wash at the kitchen sink and the toilet was out in the backyard.

We sat at Dad's desk with the bookcase on top. Dad flicked through the pages of the test booklet, asking me questions. It was difficult to think about sums. Mum said Dad didn't want me, that he wanted a boy and he was disappointed I'm a girl. She said Kathleen was his favourite, but it was me that he was teaching the piano and coaching for the eleven-plus. It was me that he took swimming with the Labour Club and to the dock to see the navvy hut where Great-granddad lived.

130

'A penny for them, Girlie! Come on, concentrate. Now then. The report from your new school, Vicarage Lane Juniors, says you have a reading age of seventeen.'

'I'm not top of the class, I only came third.'

'Third out of a class of forty-four, Girlie, that's good. We'll just practise your sums a bit more. You have to be quick in your mental arithmetic test and it's important to be able to add up the cost of what you buy. Now then, if 36 packets of biscuits cost £1.16s.0d, how much do 35 cost?'

'Easy. £1.16s.0d is 36 shillings that's a shilling each. So 35 will cost 35 shillings, that's £1.15s.0d.'

We went through several pages of the booklet, Dad asking questions, trying to catch me out and unable to hide his pride when he didn't. It was nice being close to Dad, watching his huge, weather-brown hands fumbling to turn the pages, smelling his strange mixture of soap and sweat.

Mum appeared at the doorway with her usual smile for Dad and, when he wasn't looking, a scowl for me. She couldn't touch me here and she knew it.

'The girls are in bed now, waiting for you to say goodnight.'

Dad got up to go. I broke inside like a china doll dropped onto the floor. Mother grinned. She was almost purring like one of her cats. Perhaps Dad did love Kathleen most.

He paused at the door. 'Don't worry, Girlie. You keep this up and you'll pass your eleven-plus with flying colours.'

Although he didn't say it, I knew it was me he was proud of.

Sunday 6th September 1992, Oxford, U.K.

A month ago, not having heard from Jon and Dan, I sent them a 'lazy letter' where they only have to fill in the blanks. This is their reply.

Dear Jon and Dan,

I am not very pleased that I have not had a single letter from you even though I have been here for a month now and have sent three letters to you. Please complete the form below:

Dear Mum/00Mum

1. I am sorry I haven't written. I forgot/was busy/couldn't find a pen
I shouldn't have bothered

2. I am well/sick/tired/in jail
stupid

3. My work is going well/ I haven't got a job yet/I've been sacked
joined the circus

4. Dad has fixed the guttering/is waiting for the water to penetrate the walls
clearing up the water

5. Puss Puss and hamster are being looked after/neglected/dead
cooked. Dad lost his job

6. Nanna is OK/ I couldn't be bothered to phone her

7. Daniel and Mandy are: Parents

8. Jonathan is: not an uncle

9. Dad is: signed to EMI for £1m

Love from
Dad, Jon, Dan, Mandy, Puss Puss, Hamster and Big Ted

Dear Eileen,

I am enclosing the completed Lazy Letter form you sent to Jon and Dan. It was filled in before I even saw it. Some points do, however, need qualifying!

1. They haven't, in fact, written (apart from one letter from Jon that he didn't send) although I have nagged them from time to time.

3. Although Dan has been laid off, he hasn't joined the circus (unless that is the current name for the dole queue!) Jon hasn't been working lately but is lying on the sofa thinking about it.

4. You should by now have received my letters telling of the progress with the guttering.

5. Both statements are untrue to date.

6. I have communicated all news to your mum. She was well when I last spoke to her.

7. Not noticeably. (They'd better not even be prospective ones!)

8. !

9. I wish.

One or two of the signatures are genuine.

I heard on the BBC World Service that there were serious floods to the north of Kabul recently doing a lot of damage. I usually listen to BBC World Service during my break at 03:00 hours GMT, just as you are getting up I imagine.

I'll get this in the post now. Keep healthy but don't overdo the early morning jogging.

Love

Alan and household

133

Monday 7 September 1992, Mazar-i-Sharif, Afghanistan

Dear All,

Alan's letter of 21st August arrived yesterday on the first flight since the fireworks apart from the evacuation flights. I'll try to get this on the next one.

I hope Dan and Mandy are enjoying their holiday. What happened about Mandy's back? Is she OK now? Is Jon still at the dairy?

It's difficult to remember what I've told you already. Mazar is much quieter than Kabul and the news doesn't accumulate so quickly.

I am fine. I had a problem with my hearing that started when we had a near miss in Kabul. I got a sensation of pressure in my ears like you get with an airplane taking off but no amount of yawning, chewing or nose-blowing would shift it. It seems to have gradually recovered since I've been in Mazar. Yesterday I heard a strange sound and wondered what it was then realized it was the clock ticking!

Love to all,

Eileen/00Mum

Wednesday 16th September 1992, Mazar-i-Sharif, Afghanistan

Alongside other agencies, we continue to work among the displaced, whose numbers increase daily. There are 47 schools and public buildings, plus an unknown number of guesthouses and hotels, which the provincial governor has taken over to house them. The people in the schools are the worst off. Many more are in the homes of relatives and friends. It seems that every room, every corridor, every corner of the town is occupied.

We try as far as possible to coordinate our efforts and not overlap with the work that others are doing. Although the United Nations agencies carry out the greater part of the assistance because they have the resources, one day I am invited to a meeting of agency heads to discuss the crisis.

We sit on chairs placed in a circle in a posh office. The men are dressed smartly in western clothes, as befits their statuses. I'm the only woman. After a brief introduction to the meeting from the chairman, each of these anonymous men speaks in turn.

'I sent a team in last week. They report that the food ration is not sufficient. The men are asking for more food and money to buy other necessities.'

'Yes, I agree those findings. My staff reported the same issues.'

It's my turn. 'Yes, the men said they want more food and money to purchase other items.'

Nobody is really listening now, it has all been said already by others.

It's difficult to raise 'women's matters' in this company of senior male officers. I take my courage in my hands.

'We have a female member of staff who interviewed the women I.D.P.s. They are asking for somewhere private where they can wash themselves and their sanitary cloths.'

In a single movement, all eyes turn to me. I don't think these U.N. dignitaries have heard of sanitary cloths before. They are listening now.

'The women say that the men go to the mosque to wash but they can't. They want privacy to attend to their personal and feminine hygiene needs.'

There's a moment's silence.

'Can't Oxfam get the... "items" brought in?'

'No. The women will not be able to dispose of soiled... "items" hygienically. We don't want them discarded all over the place. It'd be better to give the women somewhere to wash their cloths as they are used to.'

'They should ask their own men to make a facility available for them. We deal with the men, the men provide for the women. That's how we work.'

'The women will be too embarrassed to mention feminine hygiene to their men,' I reply. 'They are also asking for condoms. They say that the last thing they need now is to get pregnant.'

The worthy officials grin like schoolboys sniggering at a dirty joke.

The Australian representative of the International Committee of the Red Cross speaks bluntly.

'The sanitation arrangements are appalling. It's a cholera outbreak waiting to happen. When we visited yesterday, we were up to our ankles in sh– '

'We understand,' interrupts the chairman. He looks toward me. 'Oxfam specialises in water and sanitation.'

'Yes, I did make enquiries. Unfortunately, our resources are tied up with the famine in Somalia at present.'

'Who's our U.N. sanitation engineer?' asks the chairman.

'A chap called Nyasha Jeremiah Gunda,' someone replies.

All eyes turn to me again. That rumour is still going around, then. *Ah, well.*

The influx of people has surprised the traders. They have run out of supplies and food has become scarce and expensive. There are aubergines growing in the office garden and Zia gets permission from the landlord for us to pick them. For a while, they become our staple diet. One day, Zia goes to the shops and comes back with just two potatoes.

'All I could find,' he says.

It has taken a while for market forces to kick in because the traders were afraid that in the time it takes to increase their stock, things will settle in Kabul and all the people will return, leaving them with too much stock. It is now becoming clear that the people will be here for some time and trading mechanisms are beginning to draw in the necessary supplies.

Saturday 5th September 1992, Mazar-i-Sharif, Afghanistan

I need a break, a bit of time to recover from all that has happened. I'm happy enough in my work and staying at Balkh House, it's just that a brief change of scenery would be welcome. The nearest place for getting away to is Termez, just across the border into Uzbekistan. I need a visa to go there. It's easy for the U.N. boys, they have their special *laissez passé* cards that let them go anywhere. I'm just an ordinary person without this special privilege and it's more complicated to get the necessary papers. How different from when I was young and when, from a child's viewpoint, a holiday unfolded so effortlessly.

May 1960, East Ham, London, U.K.

'What a day for seafarers! Are fourth year juniors ready for their adventure?' enquired Mr Stone, surveying us twenty children each clutching a suitcase.

'Remember, you are eleven years old now, or will be soon and people will be judging the whole school – or even all British people – by your behaviour. You will set an example of decorum.'

'Yes, Sir,' we chimed, sweetly.

'Well then, we shall set off soon. First, a register.'

Mr Stone ticked us off on his list as we boarded the coach and our luggage was stowed in the boot at the back. Then we rumbled and lurched out of East London, along the Barking Road, beyond Dartford and made for Harwich.

It was May 1960 and I was in the final year of Vicarage Lane Junior School. Every Monday morning for three months, Dad had given me a green pound note, despite Mum's, 'She doesn't deserve it.' Now the last one had been paid and duly ticked off in Mr Stone's book and I was going to Amsterdam for the half-term holiday. This was my first trip away from England and I would see strange things, like windmills, fields of tulips and people wearing clogs. Best of all, I'd be away from home for a whole week.

The ship seemed enormous as we chugged out of the harbour, into the North Sea and it began to rock and roll as the waves crashed against its hull. Spray and wind whipped my hair from my headband. I watched the gulls following the great plume of foam bursting from the back end of the ferry.

An hour before we disembarked at the Hook of Holland, Mr Stone gathered us together.

'Holland is a country from which many people, who now think of themselves as English, first came. The Dutch Queen, Wilhelmina, fled to England during the war. Her daughter, Juliana, is the Queen now.

'Queen Juliana had German measles when she was expecting and her baby was born blind. Remember that, children, especially girls. Try to catch all your childhood illnesses – measles, mumps, chicken pox, German measles – while you are young.'

Mr Stone looked more relaxed on the ship. He didn't seem to have his cane with him and the boys were cheekier.

'Sir, my dad went to Holland in the war to help the Dutch resistance. He lived in a windmill by a canal. There wasn't any cheese and he was so hungry he ate tulips,' called out Peter Veldman, without even raising his hand.

'Well, Veldman, your father was lucky to have tulips to eat. I was shot down over France and spent the last months of the war in Auschwitz. I'm only alive today because the war ended before I died of starvation. Yes, we shall see windmills, canals too and cheese is available, especially for you, every breakfast-time. Now, let's get on. The Dutch are great canal builders and they reclaimed much of their land from the sea centuries ago,

138

in fact their engineers helped Cromwell drain East Anglia, once he had cut off King Charles' head of course.'

Nobody knew so much about the history of the world as Mr Stone, even if he was the scariest teacher ever.

The hotel was a tall, old house and we went out in the coach to a different place every day, driving on roads that were once under the sea. We visited Edam where we tasted the cheese. We saw tulip fields and a place where they made wooden clogs. I bought some little ones as a souvenir. My favourite was the miniature town where all the houses were tiny and there was even a little airport where a pilot's voice spoke to the tiny control tower in English.

One evening, Mr Stone took us out onto the street. He explained that during the war the Germans had occupied Holland. The Dutch people had suffered very badly. Today was the anniversary of the day the war ended. The Dutch would never forget this day and now everyone must be silent for two minutes to show respect. The street lights flashed amber, the traffic stopped, and there was complete stillness until the lights flashed again two minutes later.

The week flew by and it was soon time to come home. The boat trip back across the sea was a rough one, as a storm raged and every child in the class was sick, except me. I often suffered from travel sickness, and I'd taken a Kwell for the journey.

It was eleven at night when the coach stopped outside Vicarage Lane Junior School. Other children had parents waiting for them by the kerbside, greeting them with hugs and kisses and picking up their suitcases as they were unloaded. I looked around. There was nobody to meet me – no hugs, no kisses to greet my homecoming. I went to the boot end of the coach and waited for the driver to put my suitcase on the pavement. I picked it up and turned to start the walk home, half lifting, half dragging the heavy, beaten case.

A few steps along the pavement, I saw a familiar face coming toward me, smiling.

Dad took my suitcase from my hand, his eyes beaming with delight.

'It's good news, look, read this letter.'

We stopped under a streetlight and he unfolded a piece of paper. 'Can you see what it says?'

'No, Dad, the light's too dim.'

'It says you've passed your eleven-plus, you're going to the Grammar School! Well done, Girlie. I always knew you would.'

Thursday 17th September 1992, Mazar-i-Sharif, Afghanistan

'Zia, I need to start my weekly report to Michael today, what is the news from Kabul?'

'News is not good. Ceasefire is declared but people do not believe.'

'It's not working?'

'Is working, Mrs Eileen, but we think it is for forces to regroup and then they will start fighting again.'

'I wrote to Michael that we'd stay here for about one month and that's how long we've been here now.'

'People still they are leaving Kabul and coming to Mazar-i-Sharif. The authorities want to return them by force to Kabul but they refuse to go. It is better that we stay here. Please to tell Mr Michael we cannot return yet. But we must make arrangements to pay Kabul landlord, Mr Rasheed or he may give to someone else.'

'How will we do that, Zia? How can we send money to Kabul?'

Nafisa joins our discussion. 'Mr Habiburahman Dawlatzai.'

'Who's he?' I ask.

'He is nice and very polite man, a close family friend of my family,' Nafisa replies. 'He has a private business in Mazar and is going to Kabul for his trading. You have met him. He came to our Mazar office to see me. He will be helpful to carry a big cash amount of US Dollar from Mazar to Kabul to pay Kabul office rent and bring back the receipt from Kabul office landlord.'

Yet again, Zia's and Nafisa's network of connections provides the solution.

Saturday 19th September 1992, Mazar-i-Sharif, Afghanistan

'Nafisa, most of my clothes are Pakistani-style. I'd like to buy some material and get a couple of *shalwar kameez* suits made up in an Afghan style. Will you come with me and help me choose?'

Nafisa's eyes sparkle and she clasps her hands. 'Yes! I will take you to the shop of my father's cousin. He will give you best quality silk or cotton at best prices. Then I will take you to my tailor and help you choose the style. He is my mother's cousin, he will make your suits beautifully. Blue, I think, blue is best for you.'

The shopping mall feels like Christmas with displays of brightly-coloured cloth, glittering bangles and sparkling necklaces twinkling in the evening darkness. Men sell on the stalls, the women enjoying their short time out of the house. A beggar calls, *'Ya Allah!'* over a hum of chatting, joking and bargaining.

The stallholder stands barefoot on a low, carpeted platform. Nafisa and I sit down on chairs placed in front of him. He pulls a neatly folded bundle from the shelf behind him and, with an expert flourish, throws open the cloth, a pink fabric with tiny, embroidered squares. He repeats the action with material in silvery mauve, plain brown and shiny sapphire.

'This one is silk.'

Nafisa flicks her head in well-practised disdain. 'That's not silk! How much are you asking?'

'Eight hundred a metre.'

'Eight hundred? That's ridiculous!'

The stallholder points to me with his chin. 'Who's the white?'

'Don't say that, she understands. She's my guest. She's from England. One of the aid agencies.'

The stallholder exchanges conversation with Nafisa.

'Eileen, he says his cousin has also brought his family here from Kabul and they are living in this man's house. He says he has only two bedrooms and it is too much crowded.'

The stallholder signals to a boy who runs off, returning a few minutes later with two glasses of orange-coloured tea, which he hands to Nafisa and me.

'I've a pastel-green cloth here that would suit her pale complexion perfectly and it's very much in fashion, all the women are wearing it.'

'No, please, Nafisa, I don't want to buy green. My school uniform was green. I've not worn that colour since.'

'You are my cousin, you should give us a better price than to strangers.'

'I will give it to you for six hundred a metre.'

'Three hundred!' snaps Nafisa.

They finally agree on four hundred Afghanis a metre. We leave with a pastel-green fabric with a pattern of tiny white triangles and exchanging a friendly *Allah hafiz*, God protect you.

August 1960, East Ham, London, U.K.

I heard an unusual pride in my mother's voice as she told the shop assistant she wanted the grammar school uniform. The lady at the counter knew immediately what was required. After a brief enquiry as to my size, she scurried up and down her ladder, opening shiny wooden drawers, slipping in and out of the room behind. She produced the necessary items of clothing, placing each one neatly on the counter. Even underwear had to be of the prescribed type and three pairs of strong, bottle-green, cotton knickers were brought, folded and added to the pile. Everything was a size larger than I needed now so that I could grow into them.

'She'll need white ankle socks, black shoes, black plimsolls for games, a one-piece black swimsuit and a swimming cap,' said the assistant, 'but we don't stock those. The headmistress likes the girls to have a bottle-green scarf for the cold weather. This is the one most girls take.'

'*Erm*, no, thank you. I'll knit the scarf myself.'

'As you wish, Madam.'

I had never had so many new clothes before. My mother had never spent so much money before.

On the way home, Mother stopped outside the Post Office. She looked down at me as she produced a slim, crinkled booklet from her handbag.

'Listen to me. This is a savings book. Granddad Burgess has been putting in ten shillings each birthday since you were born. That means you've got five pounds ten shillings in it. Go to the counter and say you need to withdraw it all. You have to sign for it. Write your name properly. Then come straight back. Don't speak to no-one else, neither.'

Mother waited by the door. I watched as the clerk counted out the money onto the counter and pushed it across to me.

'There you are, Miss, mind how you go.'

I handed the money over to mother, who without a word, stowed it away. Never to be seen again.

When Dad came home that evening he asked me to try on my new uniform. I was entirely unaware, then, of the hours of overtime he'd worked to pay for it. The clothes felt starchy against my skin. They had the fresh smell of new material. Dad showed me how to knot my school tie. I wondered why girls had to wear shirts and ties, though I didn't question it. Then I put the clothes neatly away in the tiny wardrobe Dad had made for my little bedroom.

CHAPTER 13: TROUBLE IN THE OFFICE

Monday 21st September 1992, Mazar-i-Sharif, Afghanistan

I arrive at the office and see more sandals than usual piled outside the office door. From inside come the sounds of happy chatter. I slip off my own shoes and enter to find Ehsan, Musa and a visitor sitting with Zia and Nafisa on the red carpet. As I enter they jump to their feet. I greet Musa first and then Ehsan and tell them how happy I am to see them safe and well.

Nafisa speaks. 'Ehsan says this is Hamid, his cousin. They have brought their families from Kabul because they were worried for their safety. Ehsan would like to resume his job with us here in Mazar-i-Sharif. He asks if we could employ his cousin, Hamid, too.'

Zia says, 'Hamid can be driver. Then I will be free to manage distribution work.'

'Michael said I can recruit staff provided we stay within budget and we don't have any guards now so there's a bit to spare. OK, then, Hamid can be the driver. Please understand it's only for a few weeks until we return to Kabul, and I may ask you do other tasks as well.'

As Zia translates, their smiles tell me that Ehsan and Hamid are happy with this arrangement.

'Musa is saying his family has moved up to Mazar-i-Sharif,' says Nafisa. 'He has brought with him your suitcases from Mr Rasheed's house. He says he has come ready to work and hoping to have his old job.'

'Of course, Musa, I'm afraid we only have two rooms and one outside tap. We've been cooking outdoors on a small kerosene stove. We don't have a kitchen or *chowkidar* quarters like we had in Kabul. If you can be here in the daytime and return to your family in the evenings, that would be great. With

145

two women in the office, it will be good to have a man at the door to greet visitors, bring in the genuine callers and warn off any suspicious ones.'

As Nafisa translates my words, the huge smile on Musa's face tells me of his delight.

The necessary issues settled, it's not long until we are all chatting together as if we'd never been separated.

September 1960, East Ham, London, U.K.

The first day after the long, summer holiday was a chance for the grammar school girls to relate their holiday exploits in detail, as if they'd been apart for years. I was new, alone, and knowing nobody. I was the only girl from Vicarage Lane Juniors who had passed the eleven-plus that year.

'I'm Miss Denny and I'm your form mistress. I used to attend this school as a pupil before I studied to teach maths. You must address teachers as Miss or Mrs and then their name, never just as Miss. When any teacher enters a class, you will stand up. Do not bring money to school unless asked to do so, or it is dinner money. If you bring a purse, then make sure you attach it to your gymslip belt. Do not leave it inside your school bag.'

Miss Denny was younger than any other teacher I had ever seen, with chestnut-coloured hair and a bright blue pullover. She began to walk around the class as she spoke, looking at each girl in turn as if trying to recognise something valuable, or interesting, within their pale faces.

'Every item of clothing should have a name tag sewn into it. There will be daily homework. A homework timetable will be given to you. Keep quiet in the corridors. Do Not Run! You will be issued with a jotter after assembly, this is for rough work, not homework.'

The day was long, new and different. I was in a bigger, wider world. I climbed onto the bus home crammed with books, timetables and homework, tired but happy.

Wednesday 23rd September 1992, Oxford, U.K.

Dear Eileen,

Your letters of 26th August and 7th September arrived this week.

Mandy's back is still giving her problems. She has to take a day off work from time to time. She had an appointment with the specialist today. He's booked her for a course of physiotherapy at the John Radcliffe lasting 3 months. He suspects something is torn.

Jon doesn't get much work at the dairies these days but he has been called for one or two waiting jobs at Oxford colleges. One college requested him specifically on subsequent occasions. He doesn't seem any closer to a regular job although now Bryony is about to commence University he's a bit keener to get something more permanent, as fares will be more expensive.

Dan has signed on but doesn't qualify for unemployment benefit because some previous employer wasn't paying his stamps. He's getting income supplement but none has come my way yet. Unfortunately he ignored my advice about not using his Barclaycard for extended credit and ran up £250 on holiday, not expecting to come back to no job. I've found I'm subsidising them – and so the savings I had put by have this week all gone to keep my bank account in credit.

Your temporary deafness must have been quite worrying. Were your colleagues affected as badly? Communications must have been tricky! I hope you are back to normal now.

Lots of love,

Alan

Thursday 24*th* September 1992, Oxford, U.K.

Dear Mum,

How are you? Have you ever heard of a mystery writer called P.D. James? I was waiting at one of the colleges as an agency job and it was a function for all these writers and she was the guest of honour.

Well, while you've been away I've been attempting, not always too successfully, to do the cryptic crossword. Yesterday Malcolm came up to visit and we almost completed a puzzle. I actually did most of it.

Anyway, I heard about your going deaf and I promise you that I am also going deaf due to Dad's constant hammering of the piano keys. Even Puss Puss hides from the noise and I expect Hamster would too if he could!

Ham is still alive although he seems a lot slower. Dan fixed another hamster cage on top of the old one and I recently had to start putting his water in the top half where his nest is because he was finding the tubes rather difficult. Only joking!

See you at Christmas

Love Jon

P.S. Travels far and makes one's mark on the world (4.1.4.3).

Answer: goes a long way.

Thursday 24th September 1992, Mazar-i-Sharif, Afghanistan

'Juliet Mike, Juliet Mike, this is Delta Romeo India.'

Nafisa treads her way over the piles of Afghan currency on the floor to pick up the call.

'I need to speak with Michael.'

'He's not here, Madam. Can I help you? Over.'

'When he comes back tell him to call me.'

Nafisa looks at me with confusion written upon her face. 'We're not expecting him, Madam. Over,' says Nafisa.

148

'I'm his wife,' says the crackling voice with a bit of edge rising in its tone, 'I know he's there. Put him on.'

Nafisa passes the microphone to me.

'I'm awfully sorry, Mrs Semple, I'm afraid we're not expecting him and we don't know where he is. Could he be visiting one of the other Oxfam offices?'

Mrs Semple goes off air. Quite suddenly.

'Her battery is gone flat,' jokes Zia.

What's happening? Where is Michael? Why doesn't Mrs Semple know where he is?

Sunday 27 September 1992, Mazar-i-Sharif, Afghanistan

I don't want to name him. I'll call him *Ismail*. He reaches across to the naan bread and scrambled egg. He chews and speaks at the same time. He doesn't seem to notice the flecks of food that are spraying from his mouth.

'Michael has put me in charge of all the work in Afghanistan,' he announces.

'You mean, in project matters. He said you were coming to manage some refugee projects.'

'No, Eileen, I'm the boss of all of you and from now on you must do as I say.'

Michael gave away the work in Afghanistan, justifiably his precious baby, to someone else? It doesn't sound right to me and Michael has said nothing about Ismail taking charge of the office, that's my territory.

Ismail pushes some more naan bread into his mouth. 'Hamid, you now report to me. If anyone wants to use the vehicle, they must ask me. If I agree, I will write it in the diary. Nobody may use the vehicle unless they have booked it. Hamid, you must not drive any more. You are my assistant and I will tell you each week what your duties will be.'

Some crumbs seem to stick in Ismail's throat. He coughs them up and spits onto the floor beside him. The Afghan staff flinch at his rough manners and loud conversation.

A car backfires outside. Zia, Nafisa, Musa, Hamid, Ehsan and I involuntarily recoil while our minds process what the sound was.

'*Ha, ha-ha,* sounds like gunfire, *eh*? Shot dead by a car exhaust, *bang*!' laughs Ismail, his voice filling the room.

Nafisa brushes a tear from her face with the corner of her scarf. After lunch, she is still upset.

'Eileen, he has no right to joke about Kabul.'

I understand what she means. In some strange way, it's OK for those who were there to laugh about it while jokes from others seem insulting.

Later in the day, I hear Ismail and Musa speaking in raised voices outside. This is most unusual. In Afghan culture, to shout at someone is to dishonour him or her as well as being shameful to the person shouting. I'm about to go and investigate when Musa comes in. He's not looking his normal, cheery self.

'He says he is old man and of no use to you. He is asking you release him so he can go home to his family,' says Zia.

Something isn't right. This doesn't sound like the loyal Musa who had once said he would give his life to defend me and the Kabul office.

Zia and Musa sit down on the carpet and Nafisa brings glasses of tea.

'It was terrible, Eileen.' Nafisa speaks quickly in English so that Musa won't understand. 'Ismail is disrespecting Musa too much. He uses words I cannot tell you and says that Musa is old and useless.'

I wish I could know where I stand in this office now. Am I in a position to gainsay Ismail or not? Musa was really kind to me in Kabul. The least I can do is to support him now.

'I'm sorry, Musa, I cannot let you go. I need you to greet visitors and bring them tea and chaperone me while I talk with them. If you go, I have no-one who can do that. Zia, Ehsan and Hamid are too busy. I need you here. I'm sorry, I cannot release you. You must stay here.'

As Zia interprets my words, Musa's eyes beam and his mouth curves upward into an enormous smile. His honour is restored.

'Thank you, Mrs Eileen, thank you.'

We all rise and Musa leaves still calling his thanks.

I don't know what to do. Who is in charge – me or Ismail? If only communications with Islamabad were easier and I could contact Michael directly and privately. I don't want Oxfam's private concerns to pass through the communication systems of other agencies. It's a problem.

In the afternoon, the radio call comes from Panjao asking for more cash to be sent, I don't know which of us is responsible. We have established ways of sending the money. Ismail has his own ideas.

As usual, Zia and Ehsan have taken the dollars, converted them into huge quantities of Afghani notes and returned with the cash, a metal trunk and a strong padlock. We sit on the floor in a circle and start to count out the cash.

Ismail's voice is commanding. 'What's the point of counting it all again? It was counted at the bank, wasn't it? We're just wasting our time.'

Ismail picks up the unchecked bundles of Afghani notes and tosses them into the trunk.

'Look, the money hardly fills it. It's a waste of money sending a big trunk like this.' He produces an old cardboard box. 'Put it in here, we'll seal it up and it will be just as good.'

Zia, Nafisa and I look at each other.

'We usually send it in a trunk because it's more secure,' I say.

'Well I'm in charge now and I say we send it in the cardboard box.'

With considerable misgivings, I let him do as he wishes.

Monday 28th September 1992, Mazar-i-Sharif, Afghanistan

It's four days since the radio call from Mrs Semple and there are voices at the door. Musa brings three men into the office, Michael Semple and two Afghan men I haven't seen before. Michael hands me the pouch from Islamabad. There's a fistful of U.S. dollars and precious letters from home. Michael and the assembled staff smile at my delight as I rip open the blue airforms.

'My son's girlfriend has injured her back. Seems like she's quite poorly. My husband's been to visit his mother.'

Puzzled faces from the Afghan staff greet this remark.

'His mother lives in another town, some distance away,' I explain.

The faces remain puzzled.

Musa and Nafisa conjure up lunch from nowhere and the group sits on the red carpeted floor to enjoy Musa's best fried chicken and naan bread from the cloth laid out in the centre.

'Your wife called a few days ago, she asked for you to call Islamabad when you get here,' I explain.

Michael shrugs.

'Everyone will be out later this afternoon. You can have a bit more privacy then,' I add.

Michael has different plans for the afternoon.

'I told them not to send you, I need someone who can keep their nerve. You didn't keep me informed, I didn't know what was going on. Zia said the militia came into the office and demanded that the boxes be opened, why didn't you tell me the security situation had changed? You should have told me things had changed. And Zia and Nafisa should have been with you in the convoy, not on their own in the Suzuki. And whatever are you doing carrying on with Gunda?'

I can explain it all but the words don't come.

'You should keep a second radio battery fully charged for when the power is down. And from now on I want daily *sitors* keeping me informed of what's going on.' He pauses for a second.

'Then there's the money sent to Panjao. We've been sending it safely in locked trunks for years. You sent it in cardboard. When the box was unloaded at the other end, it was raining. It weakened the cardboard. The box broke open and the money spilled out over the ground. Until then, everyone had genuinely believed we were transporting medicine. Thanks to you, we could be refused flights in future. We picked up the bundles of notes and when we got back to the office we counted them and there were tens of thousands missing. You can't have checked it at all. If you'd even counted a random sample you'd have known.'

Then comes the most devastating blow of all, 'It's just not acceptable. I've started disciplinary proceedings against you. You'll get the paperwork from Oxford in a week or two.'

This last missile scores a direct hit. The thin paper wall of strength and defiance that I present to the world is torn down in a handful of sentences. I hear myself repeating, 'I'm sorry, I'm sorry,' like the child who was pulled from behind the sunflowers all those years ago.

Michael leaves with his two men. I sit at my desk and slump over the laptop. I don't do tears. Instead, there's just numbness, the devastating darkness of failure. I can believe he didn't realise the security situation had changed but to say I hadn't told him? I was in Kabul for less than one month and sent three reports informing him of security issues and Zia risked his life to go to the U.N. offices to send them. Perhaps Michael is angry with himself and maybe embarrassed that he hadn't updated himself on the security situation before I went into Kabul, that he relied on his journey sometime earlier when things were peaceful and people were having picnics in the Khyber Pass. Why do the words always come to me later and not at the time I need them? It's impossible to think. I'm on automatic, in a daze of robot-like oblivion.

Back in my room at Balkh House I sit motionless, numb, staring out of my bedroom window.

1962, East Ham, London, U.K.

My unheated bedroom was filled with the freezing damp of a grey January afternoon as I peered through the yellowed net curtains. A group of children was playing *tag* in the road below. Above the playful squeals, one of children shouted, 'Car!' They separated to the two sides of the pavement. A shiny, black Cortina cruised along the road between them. The children resumed their game.

One day, I'll have a car and a handsome husband. I'll have two children and I'll show them all the love that my mother has not shown me. I'll never punch them or shut them in a cupboard. Every day when they come home from school I'll...

'Done our homework then, have we? Got time to gawp out of the windows?'

'Not quite, done the maths, just doing the English.'

'Don't lie to me, I am sick of your lies, girl.'

Her eyes glared their anger. I looked for a way of escaping from the room. Mother was between me and the door. She picked up my jotter and flicked through the pages.

'No work that I can see. Do you want me to fetch the stick, is that it?'

Her stick. Four feet of quarter-inch square wood that stood rifle-hard in its place hidden behind the long curtain next to her chair in the living room.

'Your father works all the hours God sends to keep you at the grammar and you stand there taking it all for granted. I should've put you in the children's home, then you'd have got what you deserve.'

She threw the jotter onto the bed and stepped closer to me. I knew what was coming and that I couldn't avoid it. I stared defiantly into her eyes. A flash of red-hot pain seared my head as she snatched my hair.

'You think you're so clever, don't you, my girl? Well, it might impress your father but it doesn't impress me.' On the last word, she slammed my head against the wall.

'You're just a wicked, ungrateful girl!' She punctuated each of the last three words with a further bang of my head. I sensed that she was enjoying causing me discomfort. I wouldn't give her the added pleasure of seeing that it hurt. I resumed my deliberate stare deep into her eyes.

'One day I'm going to tell everyone all about you and what you do to me.' It costs another collision with the wall. It was worth it.

'How *dare* you speak to me like that, you despicable child? No one will believe you. They'll just say what a wicked girl you are for telling lies.' She shook my head by my hair and slapped my face with her other hand. My scalp was agonisingly sore and my tooth had cut my lip. I refused to cry.

A key turned in the front door. Mother rushed downstairs.

'She came home with a cut lip. She got into a fight at school and as if that's not bad enough, to get herself out of trouble she's saying I did it!'

I went back to the window and watched the children playing. Their voices were happy, playful. I felt my lip starting to swell.

No more homework was done that night. I'd think of an excuse in the morning.

Wednesday 30th September 1992, Mazar-i-Sharif, Afghanistan

'Eileen, there's a visitor for you.' I recognise Gunda's voice through the closed door.

My visitor is Pramod Unia, the Regional Manager, Michael's boss from Oxford.

I look at him for a moment, taking in the significance of his presence. Ismail's belief that he's taking over the office suddenly makes sense. This time, the words come in a torrent.

'You want me to go home.'

'I think it would be for the best.'

'Beware the Ides of March.'

'What?'

'It's happening exactly as Pat from Personnel said it would.'

'I don't understand.'

'She told me Michael doesn't want me here, you forced him to accept me.'

'That's nonsense! He came round to it.'

'She said Michael is the apple of your eye, that to you he can do no wrong. It's happening as she predicted.'

I see anger in Pram's eyes.

'She said as soon as something goes wrong, I'll get the blame and you'll throw me out.'

'She shouldn't have said that, it's outrageous, I'll complain to her manager!'

'Maybe she shouldn't. She was right, though. Yes, I should have checked the security situation myself. Equally, Michael should have checked. He didn't. We both made a mistake and I can cope with that. But when I sent him reports and *sitors* telling him what the situation was in Kabul and Zia risked his life to go out and send them, and Michael either didn't read them or ignored what I said...'

'He didn't receive them. He says none of them, not a single one, arrived.'

156

'He must have had the *sitors* because he replied to them. I told him not to bring the Islamabad staff for a workshop because of the situation. He replied that he was coming. All we had and still all we have, is a codan radio to contact the U.N. in Islamabad. Then we are reliant on their goodwill to pass the messages on. Michael could have gone to the U.N. office at any time, called us directly and discussed the issues that concerned him. He didn't and I'm being made the scapegoat, exactly as Pat from Personnel predicted would happen.'

Pram is tense. I sense that he's struggling to control his anger.

'Look, it's getting late. I need to sleep on it and I have to find somewhere to stay first.'

'There's a vacant room downstairs. You can ask Gunda. I'm sure he'd be happy for you to use it.'

In the morning Pram disappears for a while. I imagine him going to a U.N. office that has communication equipment and consulting his boss, the Overseas Director in Oxford. He looks calmer on his return. We talk again.

'You've been through things that no human being should have to go through and you're in shock. Look, you're due a week's mid-term leave. You're to take it now and outside of Afghanistan. Where do you want to go? Termez in Uzbekistan, Murree in Pakistan, or somewhere else?'

'I'd like to go to Murree. That's where my children went to school. I know some people and my way around up there.'

'Right. Book yourself on a flight out of here. You're to take the whole week and if you find you need a bit longer, just let me know.

'Thank you,' I mumble.

'You should understand that Michael has been under a lot of stress for reasons I'm not free to tell you about. He's long overdue for his home leave and I told him he must take it now. He won't be back until the New Year. By then your assignment will be completed. I'll run the Islamabad office myself until he returns.'

'The disciplinary?' I stammer.

'I can see there are mitigating circumstances. I don't see anything to be gained by pursuing it.'

The fog in my mind suddenly lifts.

Saturday 3rd October 1992, Mazar-i-Sharif, Afghanistan

'It's because she's not married that she's that way,' says Ismail. 'Every time I speak to her she snaps. All my friends in the U.N. agree, it's because she's single. All women should be married. It's not natural for them to be single. And you must be very careful with her. Nafisa's a spy. She betrayed secret information about the U.N. to the Egyptian government. Don't tell her anything.'

I know from my time in Pakistan that stories of informers and accusations of spying abound, with nothing remotely resembling evidence. I take Nafisa aside.

'Nafisa, you've mentioned to me a few times that you worked for the World Health Organisation.'

'*Oh*, *yes*, Eileen. I enjoyed my job too much.'

'So why did you leave it?'

'It was terrible, Eileen. My boss was having relations with his Afghan secretary. You know, for an Afghan woman to do this, it is very wrong. In some families, they would kill her. It was too much difficult for the rest of us, the other Afghan women, because we must not be seen with her. We reported it to the agency head. He took no action. We wrote to the regional office in Egypt. They investigated but also did nothing. Everything was too much tense and we who had made the complaint resigned. Then our male colleagues, who remained there, overheard conversations among the international staff saying that we were spies. It is not true, Eileen, it is not true! We did not do these things, we only complained something that in our culture is completely forbidden.'

I have my own way of finding out who is honest and who is not. Nafisa is now managing the Afghani cash and book-keeping very well. I ask Ismail to take over the U.S. dollars from me while I'm away. Before I leave for Murree, I count the cash in both tins. It agrees the running totals in the books, which I sign and date as evidence of my check. Then I slip an Afs 1,000 note into Nafisa's cash tin and $50 of my own money into Ismail's dollars tin.

They both now have more cash in their tins than their books say. I wonder what I'll find when I return?

CHAPTER 14: THE MURREE HILLS

Wednesday 7th October 1992, Mazar-i-Sharif, Afghanistan

Two good-looking young pilots skip up the steps, open the passenger doors to flight Salaam Zero One and beckon us aboard.

This U.N. flight to Islamabad is the first stage of my journey to the Murree Hills. When all are safely seated and belted, the pilots slam the passenger doors shut and take their places. It's the type of plane where the passengers sit opposite each other, knee to knee. There's no partition between the pilots' cockpit and us. The engines hammer with fury until the plane reaches V2 and the ground ducks away beneath us.

'There are some red lights outside. Looks like anti-aircraft fire. Can you confirm?' the pilot says to his radio, as calmly as if he's reading us a bedtime story.

Flight Salaam Zero One does a steep, fuselage-shaking, banked turn.

'There's a spot of bother on our route,' explains the co-pilot. 'We're making a slight detour. It will add forty minutes to our journey time. Please help yourselves to the cans of cola in the cool box by the door.'

I close my eyes. Whatever's coming at us, I don't want to see it.

Saturday 10th October 1992, Murree Hills, Pakistan

Dear All,

Am enjoying a lovely week's break up in Murree. I walked through the forest where Jon and Dan used to play. I remembered walking up Sandes Hill when they jumped down from the trees with sticks in their hands shouting *Stand and deliver!* I think that was a pop song then. I remember I obliged by being 'frightened' and gave them a few rupees each.

I visited Ian and Isobel Murray – yes, they are still here. Ian is still teaching science and Isobel in the elementary school. I said I'd like to see Jon settle down. They laughed and Isobel said, 'You're working in Afghanistan and you'd like your son to settle down?' I guess they have a point!

I'll try to phone you on Sunday. I assume you'll all be home then.

Have you repaired the gutter yet?

Look after each other.

Lots of love

Eileen/00Mum

Sunday 11th October 1992, Oxford, U.K.

Dear Eileen,

It was good to get your phone call from Murree today. I telephoned your Mum straight away. She has been hard at work in the garden.

I wonder if it is cooling down much there yet? It is colder than usual for the time of year here. My new watch gives me the temperature amongst other things. It registered 52F in my ballet class last Saturday in spite of two heaters!

Dan's job seems to be going alright. He managed to get his boss to put the job offer details in writing this time after his experience of working at a hotel for a week unpaid!

Last week I put in a request for 2 weeks' holiday in the new year so we can go somewhere together. The works' manager said that although it wouldn't normally be allowed immediately after the Christmas week, the circumstances were somewhat special and he would see what he could do. His superior, however, was anxious not to set a precedent and could only allow the second week of January. Seeing my look of utter dejection must have had an effect because he later came back with the offer of a deferred payment holiday week prior to the agreed week so all is well.

I've replaced the pane of glass in the kitchen door (which Dan broke because he'd forgotten his key yet again) with clear plastic and put in a new cat flap. Puss Puss has been through it several times although she doesn't know it because her mind was on the salmon cat food I was tempting her with. At present she still waits patiently out in the conservatory while trying to look sympathetic when I beckon her through the 'glass'.

Jon missed college today. Bryony asked him to go over to Bath to see her. He phoned me from there in a terrible state, feeling dumped by Bryony saying she wanted some space until Christmas. He was extremely upset. When I picked him up from Oxford station yesterday he was a little better but didn't sleep last night worrying about it. He knocked on my door at 5 in the morning and we talked it over.

Lots of love
Alan

I'm sorry I'm not there to comfort Jon but his dad is the right person to console him because, a little over 20 years ago, it was Alan who was the broken-hearted young man.

October 1969, Trinity College of Music, London, U.K.

He looked a million miles away, sitting alone in the lecture room and staring out of the window. It was nearly Christmas and the streets outside Trinity College of Music, London, were packed with shivering shoppers. A symphony of rumbling engines and roaring exhausts from the Marylebone Road was blending in an absurd harmony with the Trout Quintet playing from a room upstairs.

'Hello, is this where the baroque lecture's going to be at ten?'

'*Oh, erm,* yes,' he replied.

I had recognised him the first time I saw him. Alan Masters, the boy I'd seen on TV in the *Tonight* show, the one from the musical family that did the charity concerts. With his blond hair and blue eyes, he looked even more handsome in the flesh than under the TV lights.

As I walked toward a seat, I noticed his face. He didn't seem 'with it' somehow.

'Are you alright? You look... Oh, sorry, I shouldn't pry.'

Embarrassed, I took a score from my bag and pretended to study it until he turned toward me and it all came tumbling out.

'...and she gave me back the ring and said, "I don't want to marry you, Alan, I'm sorry," and walked off back inside her house. Now she won't answer my letters, or the telephone and she won't see me.'

'I used to see a boy. He was nice. The trouble is, sometimes things change. It's hard to say it, so you...'

Two other students breezed into the room. I didn't want to embarrass him by speaking about it in front of them.

Alan stayed sitting next to me as the lecture droned on. I could see he wasn't concentrating, his pen drawing odd-shaped rings on his notebook, his mind somewhere else entirely.

Over the next few weeks, I noticed him more and more. In the common room, at lectures, in the canteen, Alan just always seemed to be where I was.

I was sipping a cup of vending machine coffee when he came and sat at the table with me.

'I, *erm*, I thought I'd like to go to the cinema on Saturday. I was wondering... I thought maybe... Would you, *erm*, like to, well, come with me?'

It took a moment for me to take it in. The most handsome man in the college was actually asking me out.

Alan leaned back in his seat. 'No, I can see you think it's a bad idea. Sorry, I... *erm...*'

'No, yes, I mean, it's not a bad idea. I'd love to come. To go to the cinema with you.' Damn my inability to say the right thing.

'*Ben Hur* is on, or the *Sound of Music*?'

'Oh, it has to be the *Sound of Music*, doesn't it? For us?'

After the *Sound of Music*, we were seldom apart. We sat together in lectures, ate our lunch together in the canteen and talked together in the common room. I had never known anyone as handsome or as musical.

Six months later, inside Fellowship House, the student hostel where I was staying, I was ready, waiting, wearing my warmest coat. Hearing the buzz of the Honda's distinctive toy-like horn, I put on my headscarf and stepped outside into the drizzling rain.

I climbed onto the back seat and wrapped my arms around his waist. He glanced over his shoulder at the traffic and the moped bounced away on its shallow suspension over the manhole covers and badly-mended junctions as we rode off into the London twilight.

'Cod and chips twice,' announced the café man placing in front of us two plates of piping-hot fish and chips, fresh from the fryer.

The food began to thaw my wind-chilled body.

Alan glanced at my rain-soaked headscarf hanging over the back of the seat next to me.

'There's always a price to pay with motorbiking – bad hair and wet clothes. Never mind, we'll have a car one day, a Reliant Robin.'

'That only has three wheels, doesn't it?'

'Yes, but I can drive one on my motorbike licence.'

'That'd be nice. We could go to the seaside at weekends.'

'Yes, or go and see Wales, it really is beautiful up there.'

'I suppose it's too far to go on the scooter.'

'We could take the bike with us on the train,' Alan replied, 'use it for touring when we get there.'

It made me giggle. 'Are you inviting me to a Welsh holiday?'

'Listen, Eileen, I want you to know... *erm*, I want to say... I... would like to visit North Wales with you... on our honeymoon.'

I felt a timpani beat pound inside my body.

'I, *erm*, I want to marry you, Eileen Hayward, if you'll have me...'

The man at the next table and the café man were grinning at us. I was sure they were listening.

Alan drummed his fingers on the table in time to a tune in his head.

'I'll compose the introit. What about a fanfare in F major, to announce to everyone I love you?'

'F can be flat,' I joked.

Alan groaned at the pun.

'Do I take that as a *yes,* Eileen Hayward?'

'You most certainly do, Alan Masters, you most certainly do.'

Thursday 15th October 1992, Mazar-i-Sharif, Afghanistan

Returning to the Mazar-i-Sharif office from Murree, the first thing I want to do is check the books. Will Nafisa declare the Afs 1,000 or Ismail the $50 that I slipped into the cash tins to test them?

Nafisa looks distraught. 'Eileen, I have searched and searched. I cannot find my mistake. There are 1,000 Afghanis too many in the tin. What shall I do? I am too much upset. How I can make such a mistake?'

I feel sorry for Nafisa. I can't tell her yet about the cash from my own purse that I put into the tin to test her honesty. I show her how to write the difference into the book to declare an error. She has passed her test.

I turn to Ismail. 'Are there any problems with the dollars?'

'No, everything is fine.'

This isn't the correct answer. He should be telling me that there is $50 too much cash, the amount I slipped into the tin from my purse before I left.

'Have you checked that the dollars in the tin agree with the balance in the cash book?'

'Yes, I did that yesterday.'

'Yesterday? And the cash in the tin is correct?'

'Yes, it's totally correct. Check it if you like.'

I check the dollars. The amount in the tin agrees the amount shown in the cash book. The $50 I added from my purse has disappeared. Ismail has failed his test.

October 1992, Oxford, U.K.

Birthday greetings from Alan

Dear Eileen,

Happy birthday! if you haven't already had it by the time this reaches you. I hope you get the cards sent via Islamabad.

It has turned quite chilly here since the recent heavy rains and of course Christmas has reared its mercenary head in the shops already. I also noticed a lot of Jiffy lemons in Sainsbury's today – presumably for Pancake Tuesday in February! The central heating is on and everybody we know has got a cold.

This week has been quite eventful. One of my workmates pointed out an ad for an experienced baker in the Sits Vac page of the *Oxford Mail*. I showed it to Dan. He phoned in the afternoon, was interviewed in the evening and began work last night. It's the best he's had yet – 40 hours at £200 per week and the status of a baker.

Mandy returned on Saturday from a week with her parents. She has given up her job because of her back trouble.

Last week Jon "came to himself" and went to the careers office. On their advice he has enrolled for a full-time 'A' level course with a view to going to university afterwards. They are also advising him how to go about paying for the course. I think he may still have to get a weekend or holiday job although he'd prefer not to.

Take care – lots of love,

Alan

October 1992, Toynton, Lincolnshire, U.K.

Birthday greetings from my mother

Dear Eileen,

Well you certainly move around. Alan phoned with your news. The rockit noise sounds like the doodle bugs and rockits during the air raids in the war a lot of noise but the silence at the end was the worse.

What sort of weather have you got in your place will it get very cold in the winter?

I thought I better send this card as I dont know how long it will take to get to you. Youll have to make youself a cake.

The weather has got a bit colder and weve had a lot of rain still get a drought though so they say.

Went into Spilsby this morning and had a look round the market. There were a lot of holiday makers in.

Did I tell you they are thinking again of putting a footpath along here they also want to widen the road outside here and get rid of the blind bend. It means we will lose a good bit of ground in the front. They are suppose to pay for it but it wont be much I dont suppose.

Well run out of space so will close. Mind how you go.

Mum

October 1992, Bournemouth, U.K.

Birthday Greetings from Mum-in-Law

Dear Eileen,

For weeks I have been meaning to write to you and haven't succeeded but as your birthday draws near I hope this will arrive in time to bring my greetings and wishes for a happy day albeit in somewhat different surroundings from usual. I hope you are keeping well and not too overworked. I heard from Alan that he was able to speak to you in Murree for ten minutes last week – that must have been great for you both. He said you were having a week's break. I trust you had a relaxing and refreshing time.

It's a pity that Alan has such long hours in his factory job – he had a heavy cold when I rang last weekend – but at least it is employment in these uncertain days.

Alan told me that Daniel had had an interview for a bakery job and had been accepted – better pay and shorter hours, also that Jonathan was going to study for more A-levels.

The weather is turning colder now – September was a very wet month.

Well, it's time to get ready for my four piano pupils. Many happy returns of 20th and take care!

Much love

Mum Masters

October 1992, Oxford, U.K.

Birthday Greetings from Dan and Mandy

To Mum

Happy birthday. Lost my job the day after we got back from holiday. Had used nearly all my credit card limit up. We are moving into a bedsit near where the bakery will be moving to. Mandy had to give up her job cos of her back problems.

Take care, Love, Dan and Mandy

October 1992, Oxford, U.K.

Birthday Greetings from Jon

I open Jon's card to find a hand-drawn picture of a blazing Kabul. Underneath the flames a woman wearing a *hijab* scarf and a cartoon of me are standing over a birthday cake with an unlit candle in the middle. The woman is saying, 'That's all very well, Eileen, but where do we find a match?'

Tuesday 20th October 1992, Mazar-i-Sharif, Afghanistan

Gunda enthusiastically scrapes the last spot of gravy from his plate then licks it off his fork. 'You've got to have a party.'

'I don't know. I'm a bit old for that sort of thing.'

'Rubbish. My grandmother had a birthday party when she was sixty. We'll have it at the Staff House. They've got a stock of lager to liven things up. They can do food as well. I'll ask them.'

'OK but I'll pay for it.' I take some dollars from my handbag and give them to him.

'Every little thing will be alright,' he sings, bouncing away to organise it.

Saturday 24th October 1992 Mazar-i-Sharif Afghanistan

'What music do you like?' asks Gunda blowing the dust off the amplifier he's setting up at the U.N. Staff House for my birthday party.

'I don't know. Anything you like.'

'What about...'

CRASH!

A deafening blast forces the windows open, a sound familiar from Kabul. One we haven't heard in Mazar-i-Sharif before.

Gunda reaches for his walkie-talkie. 'What...? Where...? Any casualties...?'

After three calls he relays the information he's gathered. A missile has hit a winter fuel container.

'It's only a stray rocket and no casualties. They've declared a security alert. Unfortunately, it means some people won't be able to come,' he explains.

I remember Zia and Ehsan going at night to bury our own supply of fuel in the office garden.

'Can't be stolen easily and safe from rockets,' Zia said. Now I see what he meant.

'Come on everyone, dance!' urges the unceasingly energetic Gunda, turning up the music. Despite the security alert, twenty-five people have come to the party. There's plenty of food for everyone, savoury and sweet rice dishes. The Staff House, by special concession, stocks cans of lager, which are consumed in large quantities.

There are only four women. The men dance with each other, taking it in turns to dance with us girls.

One man sits alone at the bar. He's the security officer on alert. If the security situation were to deteriorate, he would be responsible for getting us all into bunkers. While on duty, he's not allowed to participate in the festivities.

'Poor chap,' comments Gunda. 'Come on, let's dance!'

1964, East Ham, London, U.K.

My fifteenth birthday marked the day when I could have a Saturday job. I walked along High Street North calling in at each shop to ask whether they had any Saturday jobs. I came to Woolworth's. I approached a lady at the record counter and she called the supervisor, who called the manager. I was taken on to start on Saturday.

This was before the days of self-service and staff were allocated to a specific counter. I was put on shoes: selling plimsolls, shoe polish, rubber soles for mending shoes, and steel caps for repairing stiletto heels.

On my first day, the supervisor took me to a till and showed me how to ring up the correct total. In those days the tills didn't do the adding up. You had to add it up yourself and ring in the total. She showed me how to count out the change.

'It cost two shillings and tuppence. The customer's given you a ten shilling note. First take out the change to make it up to half a crown.'

I took out fourpence.

'Now make it up to five shillings.'

I took out half a crown.

'Now make it up to ten shillings.'

I took out another two half-crowns.

One demonstration. That was it. I was put on the shoe counter with Mrs Gates. Mrs Gates taught me how to keep the counter clean, tidy and stocked with items from the upstairs stock room. If a customer asked for a size that wasn't out on the counter, I would be sent upstairs to the stock room to find the correct size. There was no chair to sit down on, sitting down meant you were not working and if you were not working, you were not needed.

At the end of the day, when the shop was cleared of customers, everyone stood by their tills as the supervisors came and collected the contents of the tills, each packaged in a cloth bag with the till number on it. At six o'clock, when all the bags had been collected, the staff were allowed to go. I went upstairs and collected my coat and handbag. My feet were throbbing. I hoped I'd get a seat on the bus home.

As I passed the pie and eel shop on the way to the bus stop, the smell of fresh pies was irresistible. I went in and asked for a meal at the clean, marble counter. It was the Londoners' secret favourite – pie and mash and green liquor. I opened my wage packet and took out a shilling and a sixpence. Sitting down at one of the tables, I realised for the first time that a day on my feet had given me an appetite. As I tucked into the hot pie, it wasn't the only flavour I enjoyed that day. I had discovered the most satisfying taste of all – my independence.

CHAPTER 15: ECHOES OF CONFLICT

Monday 26th October 1992, Oxford, U.K.

Dear Eileen,

How are you doing? There's not a lot to report here except that Jon has had a bad week on the romance front. He doesn't know what to do with himself. He hasn't been concentrating on college work and is getting quite depressed. Yesterday we had a long chat about everything and he seems a bit better today.

Dan now has the keys of his bakery! (I hope he has better luck with them than he's had with the house keys!) His bakery is moving a little way out of Oxford. We're not sure where that is but Dan and Mandy hope to go and get a flat share not far from it. Today they have gone to bank Dan's first pay cheque from his new job. The agency has managed to sort out some money for the time Dan was working at the hotel in Woodstock. The hotel had him continue to work beyond the agency's contract but didn't pay him at the end of the fortnight.

Friday – it's a red letter day today! Dan paid some keep – the first in four months. I was positive about it. This letter has taken a week to write so I'd better post it.

Lots of love,

Alan.

P.S. It was Mandy's 18th birthday today. I bought her a clock from us but I will get her some more bits and pieces when I see what they need in their bedsit.

Wednesday 4th November 1992, Mazar-i-Sharif, Afghanistan

A turn in the weather accompanies my late October birthday celebrations. Since Musa brought my luggage from Kabul, my room is cosy despite the approaching winter. A plastic sheet over the window keeps out the cold draughts. I'm using my electric blanket, the sort you can keep on all night and the duvet I brought with me. With an electric heater, my travel jug and candles for when the electricity's off, a supply of books and my radio tuned to BBC World Service, I'm ready for the winter.

One night, a loud roaring intrudes upon my sleep. I glance at my bedside clock. It's three in the morning. A sinister thunder is vibrating overhead, sweeping across the top of the house. I can hear Gunda and the others coming out of their rooms and calling up their colleagues on their walkie-talkies. I leave my warm bed, shivering in the cold bedroom. Should I dress? Is this the signal that it's time to leave? My emergency bag is permanently packed, ready for leaving at a moment's notice. Has that time come?

The overhead roar passes. I hear the conversation downstairs dying away and the boys returning to their rooms. Should I try to get back to sleep or stay awake and alert? I go back to bed and doze fitfully, telling myself to stay calm, to quench the anxiety.

By breakfast the next morning the U.N. boys have pieced together the news of what happened. They say that Heckmatyar, the Mujahedeen commander in charge of Herat, threatened to rocket Mazar-i-Sharif, which is under the control of Commander Dostum. What we heard was the roar of a fleet of MIG bombers taking off from Mazar-i-Sharif airport heading for Herat, where they bombed the airstrip to prevent Heckmatyar sending his rockets in our direction.

I don't know how long it takes to repair an airstrip.

Sunday 8th November 1992, Oxford, U.K.

Dear Eileen,

I phoned your mum today to update her on your news. She has been hard at work in the garden. Today she was installing a power socket in her shed. It's for her new shredder. She says she's got about 20 bags of twigs and branches to feed into it. I could do with one here. I've accumulated half a dozen bags from my initial attack on the front garden and there's still more.

I drove Dan and Mandy and their belongings to their new flat today. I hope they are able to get used to it. Dan arranged it all with a friend of a friend. Mandy saw it for the first time today. It is a small 3-bedroom semi in which they have one room. They share the house with the (single) landlord and a couple. It is very basic – one bathroom/toilet, a small kitchen with twin-tub (that Mandy doesn't know how to use!) One fridge with a small ice compartment packed full already. There's no telly so they'll need a licence for their portable. I may get that for them. In short it is a drastic comedown from here. On the positive side, which I tried to emphasise, it is ten minutes' walk from where his bakery will shortly be moving to. So Dan won't have any fares. They should be able to save and look around.

I felt sorry for Mandy as we filled all the space around their bed with all their belongings and when they shopped at their local Spar shop for meals that were suitable where no freezer space or microwave is available. I assured them that they could come and stay or visit us whenever they wanted.

Jon is still in the doldrums. He's still missing Bryony and wishing they hadn't broken up. I'm sorry he has to come home to an empty house during the week because of my hours. At least he seems to be making social arrangements with college friends at the weekends. I'm trying to encourage him to go back to college and get stuck in.

We received your letter of 23.10.92. Glad you had a happy birthday. I trust you remembered your cha cha cha.

Lots of love and keep away from the windows!

Alan, Jon, Dan and Mandy

175

Saturday 14 November 1992, Oxford, U.K.

Dear Eileen,

How are you doing?

We got your letter of 27th October this week. We're glad it is quiet there. There hasn't been anything in the news from Affy here.

Dan and Mandy bought a second-hand fridge for their bedsit for a tenner. They don't have a Sainsbury's near them so they asked me to drive them to our Sainsbury's on Friday evening. They spent half as much again as I did for Jon and myself. I think the checkout bill came as a bit of a shock to them!

If you haven't heard already, the Anglican Synod has voted in favour of the ordination of women priests. There's another 1% bank rate cut (now 7%) – lowest for 15 years.

I seem to have run out of news. I will stop writing now as the bedroom floor is littered with bits of correspondence which need my attention.

Lots of love

Alan and Jon (and Dan and Mandy in their absence).

Saturday 14 November 1992, Mazar-i-Sharif, Afghanistan

'We need medicines, urgently. Our usual order, over.'

'I'm sorry, Murali, we cannot fill your order at the moment. All supplies are in Kilo location. We are now in Mike location. Over.'

'Eileen, this is urgent. Please go to the supplier and obtain what we need. If you haven't any Afghan medicine, send us Pakistani, or even American medicine. Over.'

'I understand, Murali but there are no supplies available where we are now. We'll send you what we have while we try to resolve the situation. Over.'

Sitting on the floor with my legs curled to one side is killing my knees. I'd like to stretch my feet forward. Unfortunately,

176

that would be terribly bad manners. I put down the microphone and make a note of the call in the radio logbook:

14 November 1992 13:35 hrs
From Murali in Panjao
Request for top up funds for Panjao relief programme.
Explained unable to supply at present time due to money still being in Kabul bank. Undertook to resolve asap.

In the room that serves as our Oxfam office, Nafisa is sitting opposite me, cross-legged on one of the garish red mattresses that line the walls in place of furniture. Pen in hand, books and papers scattered around her, she makes an entry in the cashbook and looks up. 'Eileen, we have one hundred and twenty dollars left.'

'Zia, is there any way we can get the money transferred from the Oxfam account in Kabul to a bank here in Mazar-i-Sharif?'

'No, Mrs Eileen. We must go to Kabul and withdraw money. Is no other way.'

Oh, no. Not Kabul. Being there the first time was bad enough. Going back?

'Then we must bring in office. If we deposit in bank, they will keep. There is shortage of money because of bombing and banks do not want to give.'

'So we have to return to Kabul to withdraw the money, not knowing if they will let us have it?'

'Yes, but I have cousin works in bank, he will help us.'

'Zia, is it possible to fly to Kabul? I really don't want another long road journey.'

'I have uncle works in Ariana airline office. He will help us buy tickets.'

This time, Zia and I go to the U.N. offices to enquire about the security situation in Kabul before we set off.

'It should be OK,' the security officer says cheerfully, 'only five rockets and nine dead were reported yesterday.'

Is that news scary or reassuring?

Monday 16th November 1992, Mazar-i-Sharif, Afghanistan

As I leave the house that morning, Gunda and his motley crew of tenants solemnly line up, shake my hand and wish me luck.

'Good luck, Eileen.'

'Yes, good luck, be careful.'

'Hope it all goes well.'

'Come back safely.'

I meet Zia at the office and we set off in the Suzuki, driven by Hamid.

Outside a drab airport building, we get down and I lift out my travel bag. Zia, dressed as usual in smart western-style trousers and shirt, doesn't have an overnight bag. I suppose he'll borrow anything he needs from his cousin in Kabul.

We go to a window and Zia presents our tickets and ID papers. The desk clerk says the flight will go today. He doesn't know when.

Mazar-i-Sharif airport consists of a few dilapidated buildings and a network of crudely repaired runways. The wreckage of shot-down planes has been pushed to the sides, eerie reminders of the airport's explosive past.

The plane arrives. Its engines become silent and the propellers slow to a stop. It discharges its passengers. Two pilots emerge and go into the building.

After the pilots' lunch break, we are allowed to board. Zia sits by the window. I prefer the aisle seat. We feel the vibration of the wheels against the rough ground as the plane taxis to the holding point and the thrust of full power as it accelerates up the runway. We rise into the air. Instead of the usual 'the emergency exits are there, and there,' instructions from the stewards, the pilot leads the passengers in the Travellers' Prayer from the Qur'an.

Memories of Kabul explode in my mind, when artillery shells thundered down from the hills shredding the overcast sky into uncountable pieces and the earth trembled as rockets boomed, swished and crashed around us. The memories remain embedded deep within me, shards of red-hot shrapnel in my mind, the burning detritus of war that cannot be extinguished.

I take a deep breath, relax my tensed-up shoulders. I glance across at Zia. He's staring out of the window. *Is he feeling the same?*

Monday 16th November 1992, Kabul, Afghanistan

Under the *Foreign Payments* sign I see Razia, wrapped up like a parcel in her shawl that matches the colour of the desk at which she sits. She catches my eye and beckons me over with a nod. A man in a grey *shalwar* suit brings a chair, followed a few moments later by two glasses of tea.

'We need something to keep us warm,' Razia says. She slides her chair backwards. Under her desk, there's a single-bar electric heater.

'Usually, I have this but power is off. It is so cold now and no heat, *huh*!'

I ask her whether the bank is busy these days.

'Is little foreign business, too few foreigners in city now. Is often no electricity and I cannot do money transfer. Bank is too quiet.'

Zia comes over for my signature on some documents. 'Mrs Eileen, here is not enough money. They send to other banks to find more.'

Razia offers Zia tea. He smiles a polite refusal, returns to the counter and chats to the other men patiently waiting there.

It takes almost an hour to withdraw the money. Zia returns, still smiling despite the many setbacks. I thank Razia for the tea and conversation and we leave.

There is one more thing I'd like to do.

'Zia, I would like to go to the office and check that everything is secure.'

'No, Mrs Eileen. My cousin says there was direct hit by rocket. Then there was looting. Everything is gone. Mr Rasheed is claiming money from Oxfam for his losses. If he sees you, he will argue. Is best you don't go there.'

'It wasn't our fault. We didn't send the missile!'

'He put sleeping mats, pillows and blankets, plates and other things for Mr Michael's workshop. He is unhappy that we did not use and then it is hit. He wants the compensation.'

'He knew we were leaving for Mazar-i-Sharif. Why did he put those things in there knowing we were somewhere else?'

Zia shrugs. 'We must go to our homes now, before it is dark.'

'Can we get a bus or a taxi?'

'Bus and taxi are difficult to find. We can walk.'

There are no road signs. No side in the conflict wants to aid another by helping them navigate the area. We weave our way on foot through the labyrinthine streets relying on Zia's Ariadne knowledge of the city. In the November chill, people huddle under their shawls, children rub their hands and stamp their feet to keep warm. Each tree-lined avenue holds its charred ruin – a family home, an apartment block, a shop - now lying broken like fallen sandcastles on the beach or standing empty-eyed with the windows blown out from between fire-blackened walls.

I notice what looks like road-works except that there are two artillery guns in the centre of the digging.

'Zia, what is happening over there?'

'They have to dig guns into ground to use them.'

'They are digging-in their weapons for more fighting?'

'They are not ready yet.'

'When will they be ready?'

'Two, maybe three days.'

'Then they will fight again?'

'Yes.'

Hmm. Two, maybe three, days to get out of here. It should be long enough, provided we don't have any delays.

Zia slows his pace and looks around. I notice a small sign discreetly placed on a gatepost – two curved lines drawn to make the outline of a fish, the ancient, secret symbol, used since the time of the Roman empire wherever Christians can't practise their faith openly.

'It's here,' I say.

Zia waits while I go to knock on the door. I don't remember the names of my hosts. I'll call them George and Christine.

George opens the door. I thank Zia for his day's work and he leaves to go to his cousin's house.

In the hallway, I pull off my shawl and drop it on top of my bag. 'Did you get my radio message or are you wondering why I'm here?'

George points to the space under the stairs. 'This is our emergency refuge. We've not needed it for a fortnight now, but just in case. No, we're wondering why you're here!'

George is quite short. He has a pale complexion that contrasts with his black hair and black-rimmed spectacles. He smiles.

'Don't look so worried. Yes, the hospital office is pretty good at passing on messages.'

Christine brings me a mug of tea, made the English way. 'I'm sorry we can't offer you a bath after your journey. We've not had electricity to pump up the water since the grid was bombed at Sarobi.'

Without a trace of make-up, Christine wears her frizzy blonde hair twisted up at the back of her head. She has a competent look about her, as if she could cope with anything. I suppose that's part of being a missionary nurse.

'How are you managing?' I ask.

'I bring up a few buckets from the ground tank every day,' replies George, 'better than weight-lifting at the gym!'

Dressed in Afghan clothes, they both look thin with smiles that make their faces glow. Chris cooks rice and vegetables on a bottled-gas camping stove.

George lights an oil lamp and places it on the table. Its dancing flame creates a flickering circle of light as we eat, the kerosene smell adding flavour to our meal. George's hands are trembling slightly. His brown eyes keep darting toward Chris. Something falls down in the kitchen. He starts at the sound then looks embarrassed.

Chris smiles reassuringly. 'I don't think we'll have any trouble tonight. It's been quiet for two weeks now.'

After dinner, George invites me to join them in their evening prayers. Stillness fills the room as he reads from Psalm 91 under the yellow light of the oil lamp.

> 'Thou shalt not be afraid for the terror by night; nor for the arrow that flieth by day; nor for the pestilence that walketh in darkness; nor for the destruction that wasteth at noonday. A thousand shall fall at thy side and ten thousand at thy right hand; but it shall not come nigh thee.'

Then, out of courtesy to my hosts and admiration for their confidence in the efficacy of prayer, I set aside my agnostic reserve and recite with them the ancient intercession:

> 'Lighten our darkness, we beseech thee,
> O Lord; and by thy great mercy defend
> us from all perils and dangers of this
> night.'

George will be up late writing up the accounts by the light of the oil lamp. Chris will prepare for her work tomorrow morning. I excuse myself and go to my room. I lie on my bed wrapping the cold blankets around me like a chrysalis wraps a butterfly. Despite my tiredness, sleep does not come. Instead, the bitter coldness of the night calls up echoes of a past winter.

1965, East Ham, London, U.K.

If you stretched out your arm in front of you, you couldn't see your hand. I couldn't even see my feet. The buses stopped running. I walked the mile home from my grammar school. Thank goodness, today nobody could see me in my snobby, bottle-green uniform topped with an embarrassing beret. Cars sat abandoned at the kerbside. Even a bus stood still and lifeless in the pea-souper London smog.

After tea, I dashed upstairs, changed into my favourite yellow shift dress I'd made myself, put on a brown cardigan and ran a comb through my hair. I checked my alarm clock. It was nearly seven, time to get my skates on.

I clattered downstairs and darted into the front room to say goodbye.

'Where are you going now?' needled my mother.

'Youth club, at the church.'

'Dad, tell her, she won't listen to me. There's a freezing smog out there.'

'It's a church do, love, once a week. Better she's there with some nice boys than in some bloomin' beat club.'

I smiled at Dad. He nodded and winked at me. I grabbed my coat and hurtled off towards High Street South Methodist Church Hall.

'I wanna hold your ha-a-a-a-and, I wanna hold your hand.' I sang the Beatles' song as I walked briskly up Monmouth Road and onto the High Street, the same route I'd taken every day when I was at Vicarage Lane Juniors. Even in a total pea-souper, I knew every step of the way.

Brian would be at the youth club. I'd known him since junior school. Now he was going to the boys' grammar. He was clever. He was taking four 'A' levels. We had gone to Churchill's lying in state. We'd shivered for hours in the queue that wrapped across the London bridges and drank hot Bovril given out by the WRVS. He'd taken my hand. *Ooh,* it was like a rush of electricity right through me.

I watched my breath dissolve into the night but I didn't shiver as I walked towards the church hall. Something new and strange was sparking inside me, kissing the London air, lighting the dank, winter gloom.

Tuesday 17th November 1992 Kabul, Afghanistan

The morning air is heavy, the mountaintops disappearing into cumulonimbus. Zia and I arrive at Kabul airport well in time for our flight back to Mazar-i-Sharif only to be told that the weather conditions are not right, perhaps, *Inshallah*, if God wills, in an hour or two? We wait outside the airport building.

'Will it be OK carrying all this cash?' I ask Zia.

Our bags are stuffed with Afghani notes, enough to turn our rucksacks and shopping bags into handy seats while we wait.

'Afghan money, no problem, no-one wants. Dollars, maybe problem.'

I take the $35,000 dollars out of my handbag and turn my back to Zia. I flap around under my tunic for a moment. Then I turn, facing Zia again.

Zia casts his eyes at my enlarged waist and grins. 'Mrs Eileen, you are the Afghan woman!'

By dusk, the flight has still not happened. We return to our hosts and ask to stay another night.

Chris laughs. 'We were expecting you back. They only fly when the weather's clear.'

Oh dear. One day gone from our 'two, maybe three', days before hell breaks loose again. I do hope we get away tomorrow.

Wednesday 18th November 1992, Kabul, Afghanistan

We go to the airport again. The weather is closing in for winter, I can smell it, taste it. Zia and I stamp our feet and breathe on our hands to warm them.

From time to time, Zia makes enquiries at the window.

'Not yet, Mrs Eileen. They are saying maybe this afternoon. *Inshallah.*'

At the end of a long day, my hosts cheerfully welcome me back for a third night.

Day two of 'two, maybe three days' has gone. Only one more day to go and we'll be caught up in another round of fighting and who knows what that will bring?

Thursday 19th November 1992, Kabul, Afghanistan

Today's different. Today, we're sent inside the airport building. Yes, *inshallah*, the flight will go today.

A woman calls me aside into a cubicle to be searched. It's inevitable that she'll find the dollars. I decide that full disclosure is the most sensible option. I lift my tunic top and show her the bulging pocket sewn into my underwear. The lady searcher nods her understanding and signals with her chin that I can go through.

High above the clouds, I leave Kabul for the second time but Kabul does not leave me. For many years to come, a smell, a sound, or a word will recall its myriad voices in echoes of conflict that cannot be silenced.

Saturday 21st November 1992, Mazar-i-Sharif, Afghanistan

Back in the office, it's a relief to find that Ismail has taken himself away to the Phul-i-Kumri office, to manage some projects there, or something. Happily he has left the Suzuki and Hamid behind. He must have got a lift with someone.

I go to the radio. 'Murali, we've brought fresh supplies of medicines from Kilo location. We're dispatching five million Afghan medicines to you today. Over.'

'Really, Eileen, you shouldn't have left it so late. You've delayed our work by two weeks. It's just not good enough, over.'

'I copy you, Murali. You will have the medicines now. Over.'

'He is the long way from Kabul,' Zia says in his peace-making voice, 'he doesn't know how bad was situation.'

It's strange how one thing leads to another. Who would have thought that a simple bookkeeping task, that fell on me entirely by chance 25 years ago, would one day bring me here to this?

1967, East Ham, London, U.K.

The long summer holiday stretched ahead. In those days of full employment I could have worked the holiday in Woolworth's but five pounds a week, even in 1967, was not much for a 40-hour week. Aunt Eleanor, Dad's sister, came to the rescue. Her fiancé had died in the war and she had never married. She was now a senior manager at a small firm in Oxford Circus in central London that sold wholesale polythene products such as plastic bags and gloves.

'I need someone to do the filing. The job's yours if you want it.'

I most certainly did.

'And, *er,* while we're in the office, you'll need to call me *Miss Hayward*, no more *Aunty.*'

Every morning I met Aunt Eleanor at the bus stop at 7:30 and we took the underground to Oxford Circus. Then it was just a short walk to the office, which was located at the top of a tall building.

It was my job, every morning, to sort sales invoices, purchase invoices, letters and miscellaneous papers, find the correct cabinet drawer and file and stash away the papers. Opposite me sat Ann. She looked posh in her smart, black dress. She was something to do with sales. To my right was Mhairi from the Isle of Skye with her switchboard, a confusing array of plugs, sockets and wires.

Aunt Eleanor had her own office. The boss, Mr Shepherd, had a third office. I had hit the jackpot with this job. I was able to sit down instead of standing all day and the wage of £9.10s.0d a week was nearly twice what I could earn in Woolworth's.

One day, there was a bit of a stir. Mr Shepherd and Aunt... *Miss Hayward* were in the office having an intense conversation about the books. Apparently, the auditor was due in next week and the books hadn't even been added up. They discussed the potential of Mhairi from the Isle of Skye. No, they needed her on the switchboard. They looked at posh Ann. No, they needed her to do the sales. They looked at me.

'Can I help?' I figured that anything would be less boring than filing.

Mr Shepherd thought for a moment. 'No, I don't think so, it involves a lot of adding up.'

'What if I try it until lunch time and see how I get on?'

A discussion between Aunt... Miss Hayward and Mr Shepherd followed.

Mr Shepherd peered at me over his glasses. 'Alright but only until lunch time and see how you get on.'

'Understood.'

Aunt Eleanor placed a large book, its pages covered with handwritten numbers, in front of me.

'Add up each column and put the totals at the bottom. Then, except for the first one, add all the totals sideways. All the totals added together have to come to the same as the total at the bottom of the first column.'

I started adding up. It was easier than the eleven plus tests even though the lists of numbers were longer.

Lunch time came.

My aunt and Mr Shepherd came and inspected the book.

'It balances!' exclaimed Mr Shepherd.

'The books haven't balanced for five years. The auditor's going to wonder what's happened,' said my aunt.

I was commissioned to continue the additions for the rest of the day.

After lunch, I returned to find a small machine had been put on my desk. Similar to the till I'd used in Woolworth's, it had five sets of keys each in a different colour. There were 3 keys for farthing, halfpenny and three-farthings, 11 keys for the pence, 19 keys for the shillings and keys for tens and units of pounds. Differently from the Woolworth's till, you could enter more than one amount, pull a handle on the side and the machine clocked up the total. *Mmm...* I wasn't sure I trusted a machine to add up. I summed up the column in my head. Yes, the machine was right. This contraption seemed to work.

From that time on, they called me *the bookkeeper,* gave me a pay rise of ten shillings a week and, although I didn't know it at the time, predestined my future.

Tuesday 24th November 1992, Mazar-i-Sharif, Afghanistan

A man's voice shouts above the bubble of conversation. 'You women, you shouldn't be here, you should be at home taking care of your husbands. This is men's work.'

'We can leave, if you wish,' calls Zia, 'there are other camps we can go to but no-one else is coming to give you sleeping mats and soap.'

Another voice shouts, 'Leave them alone, they are here to help us. Don't you know what the Holy Qur'an says about helping the poor and dispossessed and showing kindness to strangers?'

The gathering moves inward. The objector disappears into the mass. It's hot and claustrophobic in the pressure of the crowd.

Zia organises the throng into a queue. 'Women and children only, please. You men stand back and let them through.'

Each morning, we load supplies onto Suzie and drive to the distribution point. Most women come with a son, as culture requires, to receive two sleeping mats and four bars of soap.

Nafisa checks a woman's ration card. 'No, you were given sleeping mats and soap last week.'

'We are eight people in our family. We need more.'

'I'm sorry, there isn't enough. You've had your ration.'

'Please, give me one more sleeping mat. I have to sleep on the bare floor with my children.'

Nafisa turns to me, 'It is too much difficult to be strict with people who have nothing.'

Zia looks up, 'We must, or only few families will have everything and others nothing at all. We only have her word that she needs another sleeping mat. Maybe her husband has sent her to ask for more, perhaps so he can sell it.'

We dare not set the precedent of breaking our own distribution decisions for fear of a flood of anguished pleas for more. Still, it hurts to turn away a woman in need of a third sleeping mat.

A woman carrying her mattresses and soap stops and stares at me. She looks familiar though I can't place her. Then I notice her eyebrows hopping up and down in a nervous tick.

'Madam, it is me, do you remember at the bank we talked and drank tea?'

'Razia?'

'Our house, too, was destroyed. My husband brought us here. We have nothing, only the clothes we escaped in.' A tear trickles down her cheek. She wipes her eyes with the corner of her shawl and disappears into the crowd.

We are settling into life in Mazar-i-Sharif, getting into a routine. Gaining acceptance by the international community has not been easy. They see Oxfam as the 'poor relation' and, compared with the resources they have at their disposal, I suppose it is. We are, however, making steady progress in our work, even as I'm nearing the end of my assignment and the time when I'll be moving on.

1968, East Ham, London, U.K.

East Ham Grammar School girls still called me names, even as we all raced towards sixth form. They noticed the threadbare cuffs on my blouses, nail-varnish-repaired stockings and unkempt hair. I felt like a sparrow trapped in a cage. Sometimes, when I was alone, I would rap my forehead against a wall to try to release the confusion and pent-up feeling inside my head.

Music concerts, school plays, recitals, I joined in, smiling, always smiling. A girl went sick and couldn't play the White Rabbit in *Alice in Wonderland,* the school's Christmas pantomime. With my quick memory, the girls asked me to step in. I pored over the script, mouthing the words to myself, spotting the cues, the memory-joggers within the other players' dialogue.

One by one we girls were called to see the deputy headmistress. Miss Cruttenden knew us well. She had taught us from when we were first years in gymslips through to our sixth form, body-conscious teenage years.

'Eileen, what do you want to do when you leave school in July?'

'I want to go to university and be a barrister.'

Her face betrayed her surprise. 'Speaking in court, in public?'

'Yes, Miss Cruttenden.'

'Girls don't do that sort of thing! You won't make university. Your father lays railway track, they wouldn't look at you. You're very good at music, why don't you do that? The music colleges are easier to get into.'

At the Methodist youth club, Brian and I sat together listening to missionaries talk of faraway worlds – seeing the sun rise in Congo, taking an oven-hot ferry ride across the Ganges. I dreamed too, though I buried those dreams for now, holding them like a slow-burning torch.

CHAPTER 16: PRAYER FOR AN INFIDEL

Sunday 15th November 1992, Mazar-i-Sharif, Afghanistan

Telemessage via Islamabad office
> TO ALAN MASTERS
> ARRIVING HEATHROW FRIDAY ELEVENTH DECEMBER ON BA FROM ISLAMABAD
> FROM EILEEN MASTERS

Sunday 29th November 1992, Oxford, U.K.

Dear Eileen,

I trust you're OK. I haven't received anything from you since the telemessage. I suppose it will all catch up soon. You should make the most of non-Christmas there because it's already started here. The Oxford decorations are in place although not lit up yet. It's mainly damp, chilly and cloudy these days and everybody has got a cold. I started cold number 3 of the season a week ago. I felt particularly bad on the Monday night shift so took the next night off to recover.

Dan and Mandy seem to be settling in at their bedsit. Dan's bakery hasn't moved yet but should do so shortly. They have very few facilities there so I invited them over here at weekends. So far they seem content with their independence.

Dan went to open up his bakery on Wednesday while his mate stayed in the car, lighting the way with the headlamps. Dan found the door already open and was met half-way up the stairs by a crowbar-wielding character. Dan wisely didn't stop to introduce himself although he momentarily wondered if it was a wind-up. He and his mate went to call the police but in the meantime the miscreants (there were two of them) made good their escape, as it were. I'm sure no stone is being left unturned to apprehend them! They didn't steal anything – well there's not much of a market for stale cakes. There's no sign yet of Dan's bakery moving over to where they're living so they are both feeling a bit down in the dumps.

Jon is getting back on his feet again after the break-up. He has started studying again. The other night he was invited out by a group of college friends to a Laser Quest match. Two teams put on electronic detecting body armour and shoot at each other with laser guns while running around trying to avoid being shot themselves. Jon was 'killed' enough times to come 17th out of 20 but his multiple deaths didn't seem to spoil the fun too much. As up to now he has always contacted his old school friends for social activities, I'm pleased that college seems to be providing new friends and I'm encouraging the process.

I finished replacing the guttering and painting the front of the house (woodwork except the front door itself plus garage door). I've given the conservatory a fresh coat of wood stain outside to protect it from the wet. We've had quite a lot of rain lately. I repaired the garage door locking mechanism, which hasn't been very secure recently.

Meanwhile, I'd better make a start on the six-month backlog of washing-up and begin scraping the grease off the kitchen walls, shovelling away the heap of free newspapers from the hallway and phoning the yellow pages for the French-polisher and art-restorer, feed Puss Puss and clean out Hamster. Only joking.

I'm planning to meet you at Heathrow off the BA flight which arrives 13:50 Friday 11th December. Whether I bring anyone depends on how much room you expect your luggage to take up. I doubt you'll know that yet. Can you telephone me from Islamabad before you leave?

Lots of love,
Alan and Jon

Wednesday 9th December 1992, Mazar-i-Sharif, Afghanistan

In my room at Balkh House, I pat the last *shalwar kameez* into my suitcase and press down the lid. After a few strategic pushes, I'm able to fasten the zip and stand it next to its companion by the door, already packed and bulging at its sides.

The months have flown by and my work is at an end. Despite the ups, downs, and even traumas, I have completed the work I was given to do within the allotted time and budget. Nafisa is the office manager now, an expert at keeping the books, controlling the supplies and managing the office.

I hear a tap at the door. Zia is exactly on time.

'Good morning, Mrs Eileen. Are you ready?'

'Good morning, Zia, yes, it's these two suitcases just here. I'll carry my handbag with me.'

While Zia carries the cases downstairs to load them onto the back of the Suzuki, I take a last look at my room. When I moved in here after camping in the office, the simple furnishings – a bed, wardrobe, table and chair, and the use of a real bathroom – had felt like luxury.

I close the door, leaving the key in the lock on the outside and go downstairs. I guess Gunda already has a new tenant lined up, another aid worker or U.N. volunteer looking for somewhere safe to stay. Tonight this will be their room with different belongings marking its loyalty to the new occupant.

The house is empty. Gunda and his tenants said their goodbyes and wished me good luck over breakfast before dashing out as usual to their offices.

I take one last look at the living-dining room, trying to impress it upon my mind in case I should otherwise forget, and follow Zia to the Suzuki.

Zia drives me to the office, unloads the suitcases and brings them inside.

I don't do any work on this last morning, I just sit at my desk turning a few pages of a file. That's the thing about my life. It's a continual flow of goodbyes and hellos. If I didn't have the sadness of goodbyes, then I wouldn't have the happiness of meeting new people and saying, *hello*. I wonder what it feels like to stay in one place, to know everything about where you are and the people around you. Sometimes, I'd like to stay where I am and circumstances cause me to move on. Sometimes, the inexplicable restlessness inside me, the overwhelming need to release myself from situations that tie me down, forces me on.

August 1968, East Ham, London, U.K.

Dad read the letter again. 'My little girlie's going to college, well I never!'

Mother busied herself in the kitchen, 'How's she going to pay for it, that's what I'd like to know.'

Dad was too full of joy to care. 'Congratulations, well done, I always knew you would. Listen, do you need to get books and things? *Yeah*, course y'do, come on.'

Dad walked briskly along the street, the letter from the college folded inside his pocket. Every few hundred yards, he stopped and chatted with a friend or neighbour.

'My kiddie's going to college, music college,' he repeated to each of them.

Mr Morris, the Methodist minister, was in the bookshop when we arrived. He grinned. 'Hello, Tom. Don't often see you in here. Buying a new Bible?'

Dad laughed. '*The opium of the masses*! My eldest kiddie's going to college, Trinity College of Music. I always wanted her to go there.'

'Well, congratulations, both of you.' Mr Morris smiled at me. 'What will you do, get lodgings or go in from home every day?'

'I'd like to find somewhere near the college.'

'When I was studying theology in London I stayed at Fellowship House. It's a student hostel run by the Methodist church.' Mr Morris tore a page from the back of his diary and scribbled a note.

'Here you are. Mention my name to the warden, Mrs Curtis, and tell her I'll give you a reference.'

I was so excited I had to stop myself jumping up and down. I mustn't upset Dad by looking too keen to get away.

'Dad, that'd save me travelling over an hour each way.'

'Alright, Girlie, if that's what you want. You're a sensible sort of girl when all's said and done but let me tell your mother, *eh*?'

It was dark except for the streetlight casting its yellow beam across his thin, teenage face. It was difficult to say. I tried to make it sound friendly.

'I mean, you're off to Bible College to become a Methodist minister. I'm going to study music… we would never really see each other.'

'We could both come home at weekends.'

'No, I'm never coming back here again, ever.'

Brian looked into my eyes. I could see he was unhappy.

We stood in silence for a moment.

'May I kiss you?' he asked.

I stood on tiptoe to meet his lips. I could hear him breathing, and felt the warmth of his body. Then, with one sweet kiss at the doorstep, we parted forever.

My younger sisters, Kathleen, Mary and Christine were in bed. Mother was watching TV. On her lap was one of the growing number of smelly, stray cats she'd taken in. Dad was reading the *Evening Standard*. I sat down. A play on the television was droning on.

Was I right to give up Brian? Perhaps we could have made it work. He looked terribly unhappy when I told him. Maybe...

Mother made a *humph* noise and peered at the television. 'I don't know why they bother putting these plays on. Waste of the licence fee.'

Hot anger welled up inside me. I hated the way she spoke.

'I'm trying to listen, it's nearly finished.'

My mother's eyes spat hatred. 'Don't you *shush* me. Apologise, you little madam, or you'll get what for!'

She brushed her cat onto the floor, grabbed her stick, got up and stood over me. I curled up on my chair.

'Go on then, Mother, hit me with your stick, show Dad what you do when he's not here.'

Dad looked up over the top of his newspaper, his eyes wide and his mouth open with astonishment.

'Did you know about this, Dad? I was only four and she gave me a vicious beating for hiding under the sunflowers. A memory I'll have all my life and it's a bad one of her.'

THWACK.

Wood upon flesh and bone.

'And she told everyone I was a liar in case I dared tell them what she was doing to me. I was only seven and nearly got the slipper at school because I couldn't say where I'd got my bruises and that it was her.'

'You wicked little liar, how dare you say things like that? You wicked child.'

THWACK.

'And she banged my head on the wall, cut my lip on my tooth, then told you I got into a fight at school. And what about my sisters, Kathleen, Mary and Christine? Why do you keep us separate? I don't even know my own sisters. Is it because you're beating them as well? You look after your cats better than you care for us.'

197

The stick came down for the third time. I reached out and grabbed it with both hands. I was wrestling my mother for it. I felt her strength through the rod as my whole body strained to seize it from her. We were equally matched. I gripped firmly as she tried to twist it away from me. Dad looked on. He seemed paralysed with shock. Then he jumped up. He was reaching for the stick. I tried to push it toward him while my mother's hands clung desperately to the last piece of her power. Dad grasped the stick. One sharp twist from his powerful, railway-labourer's hands and he wrenched it away from us both. Mother, with a ferocious glare at me, returned to her chair.

Without saying a single word, Dad snapped the stick across his knee into four pieces, walked outside and threw them into the dustbin. As calmly as if he had just put out the cat, he ambled back indoors, sat down in his armchair and carried on reading his newspaper. We watched the end of the play in silence. I was triumphant. The symbol of my childhood of fear was nothing more than a bunch of broken sticks in the dustbin.

Tomorrow, I'd be leaving for Fellowship House and Trinity College of Music. There'd be new people, a new life, maybe a new boyfriend. Tomorrow would be another world and I was determined to make it a happy one.

Wednesday 9th December 1992, Mazar-i-Sharif, Afghanistan

'What time is the flight, Eileen?' Nafisa's voice jerks me back to the present. 'Musa wants to prepare an English meal for us.'

'I don't know. They don't tell us the time for security reasons. They just tell us to be ready to go immediately when the car comes to collect us.'

Nafisa looks troubled. I ask her what's wrong.

'I worry that when you are gone, my father will not allow me to work here. It is only because you are here that he has agreed me.'

I wish I had some words of comfort for Nafisa, that I could suggest a solution. I squeeze her shoulder, the only comfort I can offer her.

The aromas of simmering rice and chicken, mixed with the smell of the kerosene stove in Musa's makeshift kitchen, signal the advent of lunch.

We sit shoeless around the tablecloth on the floor. Musa brings in his 'English special', savoury rice with flaked chicken, grated carrots and sultanas, followed by sweet rice.

'Ehsan says you will forget us when you are gone,' says Nafisa.

'Oh, no, I will never forget.'

'She will never forget rockets!' says Hamid with a grin.

'Or the bunker,' says Musa, with Nafisa interpreting. 'I sat with her for days down there.'

The others groan.

'Yes, Musa, you are hero!' Zia says in English. Everyone laughs. 'And I remember when I brought you from Peshawar to Kabul in a very harsh time; the very bad road from Torkham to Kabul, armed Mujahids were appeared everywhere and too much fear on the way to Kabul.'

'I will never forget coming to Mazar-i-Sharif in the Suzuki with Zia,' Nafisa says, 'I was too much frightened.'

'Me and you cashed big money from Afghanistan Bank in Kabul,' Zia continues, 'and you were carrying that big amount of cash. We approached Kabul Airport to fly to Mazar and after three days we could fly to Mazar. Oh God! Very difficult time was that.'

'I'll never forget any of it,' I say. Everyone laughs again.

At the end of the meal, Ehsan speaks. He wants to say a prayer for me. Hamid says he doesn't know whether it's possible to pray for an unbeliever, an infidel. Zia says I'm not fully infidel, he's seen me give alms to beggar-women. Nafisa says she's never heard me say the *Qalima* and that's what really makes you a Muslim.

Then Musa speaks. He's only a night-watchman, a travelling chef and of lower status than the others. Now, his age gives him precedence. Only Nafisa's translation sounds above the respectful silence.

'Mrs Eileen came here to help us. Day after day she sat in the bunker in Kabul as wicked men tried to destroy our city. She could have left, as many foreigners did. She had courage and stayed to help us. I also have seen her give alms to beggar-women. She is a good woman who helps the poor. We should not treat her as an unbeliever, an infidel. We should pray for her.'

It's an honour and I'm moved by it. Nafisa and I cover our heads with our scarves. Ehsan raises the palms of his hands heavenward and recites a prayer asking Almighty Allah, the Merciful, the Compassionate, to protect me and grant that I may live to see my grandchildren.

We hear the U.N. vehicle pull up outside and sound its horn. We jump up and go to the door. My two suitcases are whisked into the back of the Landcruiser. A quick two-way kiss for Nafisa, culture-defying handshakes for Ehsan, Hamid, Musa and Zia, the exchange of promises never to forget and I watch through the car window as they disappear behind me.

CHAPTER 17: RESETTING THE SENSES

Saturday 12th December 1992, Oxford, U.K.

'Where am I?' I ask sleepily.

'You're at home,' says Alan's voice.

I become conscious of the softness of the bedroom with its cream satin-look duvet cover and matching curtains, the ivory coloured wardrobe and dressing table, very different from the brown, utilitarian plainness to which I've become accustomed over the last six months.

Alan brings a cup of tea. I sip it, tasting the difference that a dash of semi-skimmed milk makes and savouring the homeliness of a forgotten flavour.

The house looks different, somehow. Downstairs, I notice how green and flowery the living room is, white wallpaper with green stems leading to small flowers and green flowery sofa and armchairs. The central heating gives a comforting kind of warmth that makes me feel I want to stay indoors, protected from the December frost outside.

I go into the kitchen. Jon's there.

'Cup of tea, Mum? I guess you didn't get much tea out there.'

I put my arms round him and give him a hug.

I have to turn myself back into a normal woman before I return to the audit office. In the afternoon comes an important part of my metamorphosis – a trip to the hairdresser's.

Christmas music jingles its encouragement to spend across the shop. With tinsel, shiny stars, red and white "snowmen", Debenhams is set out like a winter wonderland. Christmas shouts at me from all directions. My body starts to tense, to try to block it out. *Don't they know what people are going through elsewhere in the world?* I struggle to suppress the urge to scream and run out of the shop, away from the world of Christmas closing in on me. Instead, I make my way to the third floor and approach the hairdressing section. It's mercifully naked of Christmas.

'Hello, long time no see,' says Mark Anthony, my hairdresser. He takes my coat, puts it on a hanger on a rail and holds open a black gown. 'Welcome home. Did you have a good trip?'

'Yes, thank you.' It seems the right thing to say, not too demanding for him or me. He leads me to a chair and stands behind me. We both look in the mirror. He's a good-looking thirty-something, smartly dressed in black shirt and trousers, a stud in his left ear. His face has a slightly pained expression as he runs his fingers through my hair, lifting and examining it.

His face shows disapproval. 'You've been out in the sun, haven't you?'

'Yes.'

'Without a hat.'

'Yes.'

'It shows in your hair. What's happened at the back, here?'

'*Ah.* That's where I cut it myself. You know how I hate it hanging down. I decided to chop it off. Just as I was about to cut it, the lights went off and I couldn't see in the mirror.'

'And you cut it off anyway.'

'Yes.'

'Where did you go this time?'

'Afghanistan.'

'You certainly get around, don't you! Please don't take this the wrong way but you look so ordinary, no-one would ever guess what you get up to. *Hmm.* It's very dry. I'll give it an extra-rehydrating conditioner.'

'What's your news since I've been away?' I ask.

Mark seems to have done more travelling than I have in the intervening months on a trip to Australia with his partner. I try to listen, to look at the photos, to say, '*Wow!* That looks like a great trip!' but my mind won't stay in the present. It's constantly jumping back to Afghanistan, to the conflict with Michael, what I should have said to him and to Pram, like the piped music in a store constantly playing the same tunes over and over.

Monday 14th December 1992, Oxford, U.K.

There's something fresh about the ordinary things – a shower in my own bathroom, putting on a skirt, blouse, tights and medium-heeled shoes. I take the bus into Summertown and walk to the office. My shoes feel tight after wearing sandals for six months.

'How was it?' asks Philip, my audit boss. He looks different. A new hairstyle perhaps, or new glasses?

'OK,' I reply. It's the same feeling I had at the hairdresser's. I can't say what it was really like in case the person I'm speaking to isn't strong enough to hear it.

Philip wants to chat. I find it difficult to know what to say. It continues throughout the day as colleagues drop in to welcome me back. Everyone else has continued with their lives and have things in common to chat about – ordinary everyday happenings, a holiday, an evening out, Christmas shopping. I feel the months have been chopped out of my life, as if I've gone to bed in July and woken up in December. My experiences in that time have been so very different that there's no place for them in normal conversation, leaving me with nothing to say. Worse than that is my total inability to concentrate on anything. I can't reach the end of a sentence before Afghanistan snatches my thoughts away from me.

I'm walking along the High Street. I find myself glancing along the road for signs of anything suspicious, an ambush or kidnap attempt. No, everyone is going about their business. Then I remember I'm in Oxford. I hear a car door slam and it takes all my strength to stop myself curling down with my hands on my head. Someone approaches to speak to me. I haven't seen them coming. An automatic switch flicks on and I recoil. At night, in the darkness, I hear MIG bombers approaching overhead. I want to turn off the light and hide but can't reach the light switch. I wake up, terrified. I tell myself it was only a dream. I walk around the house touching the furniture and kitchen tops to assure myself that this is where I am and I'm safe.

Sunday 20th December 1992, Oxford, U.K.

It's a bitterly cold morning when the doorbell rings and I find Dan and Mandy standing on the step with two huge suitcases.

'That landlord's a conman. Do you know what he's charging us for electricity?' says Dan.

I give them both a hug and they go upstairs to their old room. Alan will help them pick up the rest of their belongings from their bedsit later.

I set a dish of roast potatoes on the table and sit down. 'Come on, everybody, eat up before it gets cold.'

I notice that Jon is unusually withdrawn. 'You OK, Jon? You seem rather quiet today.'

'*Ha!*' laughs Dan. 'He's in love with Magda, his new girlfriend he met at college last week. Nice legs. Hers, I mean, not yours, Jon!'

Jon scowls at Dan.

Dan takes the bowl of carrots and passes them to Mandy. 'You've managed to keep your head, then, Mum.'

'No, dear, this is the prosthesis I had made at Madame Tussaud's.'

Jon starts to giggle. I can't stop myself joining in. Then we're all laughing.

PROGRESS OF A KIND
POSTSCRIPT BY MICHAEL SEMPLE

Eileen's memoir is a fitting tribute to the bravery and compassion of all those people who find themselves caught up in the maelstrom of war and yet still manage to help. Eileen witnessed some of the worst days of Afghanistan's deadly factional conflict and not only survived but assisted thousands of Afghans whose life had been turned upside down.

Some say that aid agencies are more conservative and rule-bound these days than they were in 1992. But each new crisis in the world embodies many of the tensions and dilemmas which Eileen and her colleagues grappled with, not least the gaps in comprehension of the situation between those who hear the rockets and those who read about them in reports. Managers and field workers alike should read Eileen's highly personal account and then listen to each other better.

Although, regrettably, Afghans still wait for the rockets to go permanently silent in their country, I can offer a happy postscript. Zia went on to serve on the country's post-Taliban Human Rights Commission. Nafisa also works for the Commission and her parents eventually blessed her choice of the man to marry. Eventually many of the displaced people whom the team helped were able to return to their homes in Kabul. And those of the Afghan faction leaders who survived are nowadays busy making and breaking political alliances with each other rather than firing rockets. Progress of a kind.

Michael Semple
Visiting Research Professor,
Institute for the Study of Conflict Transformation and Social
Justice, Queen's University, Belfast.
October 2013

A TRIBUTE TO AID WORKERS
BY COMMISSIONER AHMAD ZIA LANGARI (ZIA)

I congratulate Ms. Eileen Masters for her amazing ability in taking notes and accurately remembering the details of all the events happened during her assignment as the Office Manager of the OXFAM office in Afghanistan, and using them now in her book *Prayer for an Infidel*.

As one of the eyewitnesses among other Afghan colleagues I found Eileen as a dedicated European's woman with high capacity of professional management ability who profoundly managed the office under the very severe armed conflict conditions that no one was sure about his or her safety. During her assignment she was not overwhelmed by too much paper works and unfamiliarity of staff with the new management system, but she was deeply concern about everyone safety and preventing them of being traumatized.

It is very difficult for an European lady to accustom herself with the horrible conflict as situation in Afghanistan in 1992, when the existence of governmental management was not visible, and the whole country was separately managed by gunmen of different warring factions, but Eileen, by her successful working under conflict situation, proved that women, as men, have the same capabilities, if women are also given equal chance as men.

Eileen's book took me back to the years 1992 to 2001, remembering how I and my esteemed colleagues were working very hard together with financial support of international organizations to provide relief materials to Afghan conflict-affected communities, including the Tajik refugees settled in Mazar-i-Sharif, mobilizing communities for reconstruction of devastated rural infrastructures and advocating for human rights of people. But never our frustration was sustained because of enjoying of everyday in serving needy people. Therefore, I think aid workers, who work under very risky conflict conditions should be appreciated.

Prayer for an Infidel, indeed, is a "journey recording book" as we have in our Persian language, called: *Safar Nama,* means journey letters, wherein the writer records the events of an age for the use of future generations, in one hand, and on the other hand, such book can be a way of tribute to those aid workers who work under very risky and difficult conditions in different problematic parts of the world.

Wishing the best of success for Eileen.

Commissioner Ahmad Zia Langari
Afghanistan Independent Human Rights Commission, Kabul
October 2013

GLOSSARY

Afghani or Afs	The currency of Afghanistan. At the time of this book there were approximately Afs 1,000 to £1
Allah hafiz or *Khuda hafiz*	*God protect you* (Goodbye)
Ariana	The national airline of Afghanistan
Bismillah	*In the name of God* used to commend speech or action to God's mercy
Bissior rocket!	*Too many rockets!*
Burqa	A garment worn in public by women that completely covers their heads, faces and bodies with a small grill over the eyes to see through
Chador	A large cotton shawl worn by women to cover their heads and upper bodies
Chappatti	A thin flatbread
Charpai	A string bed
Chowkidar	Night watchman

Codan radio	A type of radio with 2-way communication
Dari	A major language of Afghanistan closely related to Farsi
Dupatta	A long scarf worn by women, usually in colours that complement their *shalwar kameez*
E.T.A.	Estimated time of arrival
I.D.P.	Internally Displaced Person. Someone who has had to move from one part of the country to another to escape the conflict
Inshallah	*God willing*
Mujahedeen	Freedom fighters, originally of the Afghan resistance to Russian occupation
Naan bread	Leavened flatbread
Oxfam	Oxford Committee for Famine Relief
Pekol	A man's flat cap
Punjabi	The regional language of the Punjab in Pakistan
Purdah	Hidden from public view
Qalima	The Islamic creed
Shaheed	Martyr

Shalwar Kameez or *Shalwar suit*	A tunic and trousers in matching material. Men wear plain colours, sometimes with a raised collar. Women wear pastel, patterned or shiny materials
Sitor	Simplex Teletype Over Radio. A written communication transmitted by connecting a computer and a radio
UNOCA	United Nations Office for the Co-ordination of Assistance Programmes in Afghanistan
Urdu	The national language of Pakistan
Ya Allah!	*Dear God!*